Children of Incest
Whose secret is it?

Acknowledgements

This project relied on the practical involvement, good will and commitment of many people. We are especially grateful to all the participating social workers who for reasons of confidentiality must remain anonymous, but who gave freely and extensively of their time, expertise and honesty.

To the children that we never met but feel we know, we send our thanks. It is our belief that their stories will help other children to have carers and social workers more attuned to their particular individual needs and points of view.

We wish to thank the trustees of the Henderson Trust for financial support, which enabled the study to be completed. We also thank the Wilfred and Elsie Elkes' Charity Fund for their contribution towards the production costs of this book.

More specifically, our special thanks for valuable comments go to Professor Emeritus Fred Stone of Glasgow, to Professor J A Raeburn of the Inter-Disciplinary Centre for Medical Genetics at the University of Nottingham, to Professor Marilyn Strathern of the Department of Social Anthropology at the University of Cambridge, and to Dr Iris Knight, formerly Medical Adviser to a county council adoption agency. Our sincere thanks also go to Ann Wallace at the University of Dundee and to Eileen Hooper at BAAF, without whose patience and forbearance in providing secretarial support this publication would never have seen the light of day.

Children of Incest

Whose secret is it?

Alexina McWhinnie and
Daphne Batty

British
Agencies
for **A**doption
and **F**ostering

British Agencies for Adoption & Fostering
11 Southwark Street
London SE1 1RQ

Copyright ©BAAF 1993

**British Library Cataloguing in
Publication Data**
McWhinnie, Alexina M.
    Children of Incest: Whose secret is it?
    I. Title   II. Batty, Daphne
    362.7

    ISBN 1-873868-11-1

Designed by Andrew Haig & Associates

Typeset, printed and bound by
Russell Press Limited (TU)
in Great Britain

Contents

Notes on the authors

Dr Alexina McWhinnie is Senior Research Fellow in the Department of Social Work at the University of Dundee. Previously she held appointments as Senior Lecturer and a Professor of Social Work at Buckinghamshire College of Higher Education. Her professional experience in social work practice was as senior consultant/advisor on adoption and foster care in Edinburgh and as a medical and psychiatric social worker. She has researched and written widely on adoption, foster care and parenting. Her current research is an Economic and Social Research Council sponsored study of parenting in families created by in-vitro fertilisation and donor insemination (Ref. R000 231463). She was a member of the Kings Fund Centre Counselling Committee which produced the report, *Counselling for Regulated Infertility Treatments*, in January 1991 prior to the implementation of the Human Fertilisation and Embryology Act 1990.

Daphne Batty is Co-ordinating Secretary to the BAAF Medical Group, and was previously one of BAAF's Development Officers, specialising in training. Before this she managed the adoption and fostering services in two London boroughs. She keeps in direct contact with children through voluntary work in her local primary school.

Foreword

Bryan Williams

This is an unusual book about an important topic. The subject of incest attracts interest at both a popular and a professional level; but the authors are surely correct in their view that such interest typically does not add significantly to our knowledge base. The present study is grounded, not in hypothetical assertions about incest, but in the experience of its victims – children born of incest, their carers and their birth mothers. It chronicles the events and circumstances in which people learned the real facts about their origins and the impact which these revelations had on them and those responsible for telling them. In focusing on a particularly taboo aspect of family and sexual relationships, the specific characteristics of incest are distinguished from more general considerations relating to sexual abuse. The reader is reminded that not all incestuous relationships entail sexual abuse of either children or adults.

Although the original work on the study was carried out some years ago, this does not in any way reduce its topicality since little has been written on the subject of incest in the intervening period. The inclusion of a chapter discussing the genetic issues surrounding incest, written by Professor Raeburn, helps to clarify what is often the most worrying aspect for those confronting the reality of this forbidden aspect of human sexuality. Current concerns, both about adoption and child sexual abuse, by focusing on professional procedures and the rights of children, sometimes tend to oversimplify the complex moral and ethical dilemmas involved in trying to practise with a commitment to openness. The case material included here graphically illustrates how such a commitment reinforces the importance of the role of adoptive parents and foster carers and challenges the basic personal beliefs of professional workers. As the authors argue, only the incautious or the self-deceiving could claim certainty in such a complicated area. One is struck by the consistency with which fundamental concerns about personal identity and self-worth are raised in the process of disclosing the truth to those most affected.

Alexina McWhinnie and Daphne Batty, with the active participation of social workers, carers, and individuals born of incestuous relationships, have drawn together a rich collection of personal accounts. The data is not claimed to be representative in a formal sense but, given its closeness to those directly involved, the study contributes rare insights into the relevant professional and personal issues. These are drawn out and discussed by the authors in a concluding section. I am pleased that it was possible for the work of editing and summarising the case material to be carried out within the Department of Social Work at Dundee University, specialising as it does in the study of child care and protection matters. The Department has a number of very fruitful professional links with BAAF of which the present study is one tangible outcome. The reader should gain much from this unique insight into a subject about which there exists more myth than fact.

Professor Bryan Williams
Department of Social Work
University of Dundee
November 1993

Introduction

Children born of incestuous sibling relationships were acceptable in the Ptolemaic dynasty; in fact, they were viewed as desirable – they preserved the purity of the ruling family. Today, children born thus are not viewed as acceptable in most cultures. Why should this be so? Do we in the United Kingdom understand their situation? Are we still influenced by Victorian prudery? Have the new sexual freedoms made any such moralistic frissures seem outdated? What are the prevailing myths about children born of incest? What is the reality? What issues face those who parent them? What are the real issues for them living out their lives as children, as they find sexual partners and as they bear or father children?

The reality is that we can study the cultural taboos and write about them in relation to kinship groups, culture, religions, genetics, and so on. However, we know very little about the subsequent lives of the children and their parents, and the atmosphere of mystery and distrust which may surround them.

There is nothing in relevant literature that directly addresses their situation. The contemporary flood of research and writings about child sexual abuse and incest deals with the families, the perpetrators, the victims and the effects on them, whether as child, adolescent or adult. Issues surrounding the assessment of the situation, interviewing the children, the development of appropriate strategies and therapeutic programmes, the legal process, etc, are all dealt with. But nowhere is there mention of the development of the children born as a result of incestuous sexual intercourse. How do they fare? How do they deal with the secrets of their birth? Are there major health hazards for them? How many are aborted rather than allowed to be born?

This study breaks through the barrier of ignorance and silence and looks at some realities and dispels some myths. The method of inquiry is empirical, using the case studies of social workers and other practitioners who have had direct contact and experience of working with these children. The core of this book is those case histories, together with the detailed presentations of how the social workers involved had worked with these children, particularly in relation to questions such as should they be told of their incestuous origins; when should they be told and by whom; if they were told, what would be the likely outcome. These issues, however, need to be set in a wider context.

This study, therefore, offers a critical analysis of relevant academic literature on incest and examines the legal definitions of incest in English and Scottish law. A review of the literature on communication about secrets in adoption and non-biological families is also included. A specially commissioned contribution from Professor J A Raeburn, an academic clinical geneticist is the third element in the necessary context. It was written after consideration of the case material.

The format used to present this multidisciplinary material is in three parts: context, case studies, and conclusions.

PART I   CONTEXT

Chapter 1   *What is incest?*
                   This chapter considers incest in anthropological,
                   socio-biological and psychological terms; how it is
                   described in mythology and religion; what the legal
                   definitions are; and the issues of particular relevance
                   for social work practice.

Chapter 2   *Children's need for genealogical knowledge*
                   This chapter looks at the research studies which
                   underpin the knowledge that children on the whole
                   need to have access to knowledge about their origins.

Chapter 3   *The genetic factors and their disclosure*
                   This chapter considers the genetic risks for a foetus
                   and a child conceived by an incestuous relationship;
                   and the role of the clinical geneticist in unravelling
                   these in an individual case and in being available
                   for advice and counselling.

PART II	THE CASE STUDIES

Chapter 4   *The study: How it began and developed*
This chapter describes how the project was set up and developed, together with a presentation of the case studies obtained from participating social workers.

Chapters 5, 6, 7, 8   *The case studies*
These four chapters describe the social work experience of working with these children in relation to disclosure about their origins and the outcome of this.

PART III	CONCLUSIONS

Chapter 9   *Conclusions and implications for practice*
The conclusions are presented in two parts. First, the findings from the case histories and the social work intervention are presented and linked in discussion to the material in the three "context" chapters. Secondly, there is a discussion of the findings as they affect any practitioner of whatever discipline involved in counselling or advising the families of origin at the time of the pregnancy and birth of these children, the children's subsequent carers, and the children themselves as they grow to adulthood and towards parenthood.

1 What is incest?

This study is about the children born as a result of an incestuous sexual relationship. It is thus about consummated heterosexual incest. This section deals with the general question of "What is incest?", but first we have to address the contemporary confusion about the use of the word "incest" and how it is used by many writers as interchangeable with child sexual abuse. A literature search that was made early on in the study showed this vividly. Although there is an overlap between the terms, they each refer to different and specific concepts. Also very relevant is the fact that although both terms are emotive, they produce and evoke different reactions and attitudes.

Incest commonly refers to intercourse rather than other forms of sexual behaviour; it is heterosexual and defined by the relationship that already exists between the two people concerned, rather than by their relative maturity. Incest thus refers to sexual relations between certain types of relatives rather than to sexual activities between adult and child. La Fontaine explains it thus:

> 'Incest can be used with a variety of meanings. There are three main sources for the differing definitions of the term. There are dictionary definitions which rely heavily on literary evidence; there is the meaning given it in the criminal law; and there are the common understandings of most people. The three are not entirely consistent with one another.' [1]

This section develops these three themes and discusses their relevance for social work thinking.

Evidence in literature and from anthropological debate

Here we discuss what is incest in cultural terms, what is meant by taboo and the source of the strength of its prohibitions. Various explanations are available. Literature in general is full of allusions to incest; myths and legends and quotations from the Bible abound in Western culture. Other cultures and religions have their own stories and myths. (In fact everyone appears to have their own favourite example or illustration.) This section, however, will concentrate on anthropological explanations and the debate around these and how the incest taboo has been strengthened by stories of punishment, omens and witchcraft.

Anthropologists observe that human societies throughout the world formulate rules and regulations to govern and restrict sexual relations between certain kinds of relatives; incestuous relationships are those which violate such taboos.

While most acknowledge the universality of incest regulations in human society, there is considerable disagreement about how incest taboos originated, the function they perform, and why they apply to different relatives in different societies.[2] For example, the taboo exists universally between parent and child, but not always between siblings and half-siblings.

A psychological explanation of incest regulations has been offered[3] but those who present it have come up with two opposing arguments: that primary relatives have a natural sexual attraction to each other that must be controlled for the good of familial and societal survival, or that taboos arose in response to a natural aversion to close relatives – an antipathy which is either instinctive or which develops when individuals are brought up together. What neither of these arguments addresses, however, is whether the attraction or aversion is instinctual in origin or learned behaviour arising from cultural influences.

An alternative explanation derives from sociological thinking. Prohibiting sexual relations within a family prevents disruptive sexual competitiveness and offers the possibility of inter-familial alliances through seeking a mate outside the family and so achieving a social solidarity.

The reply a New Guinean is reported to have given to Margaret Mead, the anthropologist, illustrates this thinking well. To the question why marriage within the family was prohibited, he replied:

'What, you would like to marry your sister? What is the matter with you anyway? Don't you want a sister-in-law? Don't you

realise that if you marry another man's sister and another man marries your sister you will at least have two brothers-in-law, while if you marry your sister you will have none? With whom will you hunt, with whom will you garden, who will you go to visit?' [4]

A demographic foundation is given by some writers.[5] The argument runs thus. In early human populations there was probably a short lifespan, few offspring surviving to reproductive maturity, wide spacing of child births and so intra-familial breeding was unlikely if not completely impossible. Others argue that there is no conclusive evidence that the average life expectancy was so low – say to age 26 – as to preclude mating with their children.

A eugenic explanation is probably the theory with which we are most familiar in Western culture today, although whether our familiarity with this point of view is based on prejudice or accurate knowledge of the facts about the effects of "in-breeding" in humans is an issue which will be discussed again later in this book.

One argument in anthropology has made a connection between incest regulation and biological necessity, arguing that if incest were not prohibited societal continuity would be endangered.[6] With in-breeding, children with different kinds of disabilities would be produced and such offspring could have impaired reproductive capacity. Some contemporary data has supported the genetic risk to offspring and has been used as evidence for recommending abortion where there is a pregnancy involved. This needs a clinical geneticist's contribution for a reasoned debate, and this is presented in Chapter 3.

Given these various theories and views, how were taboos invented to regulate this potential in-breeding which may or may not have been recognised in all societies and cultures as deleterious? The suggestion is that the familial incest taboo was an adaptive response to the genetic results of close in-breeding and that the selection of the taboo also served to solve the problem of sexual competition within the family in a culture with an organised family life. Other alternatives would only have solved one of these problems; the incest taboo solved both. Once it existed it promoted co-operation between families which could also lead to acquiring a wider group of kinship and so have the pragmatic advantages spelt out graphically in the reported conversation with Margaret Mead.

Kinship is often seen as defined by genetic origin. Anthropologists have usually defined kinship as those relationships regarded by the actors as based on ties of substance, together with procreation, though the range of relations so defined may even overlap partially with those we would count as biological relatives. Families, however, can be defined as those related by blood or marriage.

Anthropologists still dispute the origin of the incest taboo,[7] but for our contemporary discussion it makes sense to consider it as a device which has developed and which could resolve both the short-term sociological problems of sexual competitiveness and the long-term biological ones. The biological questions raised by in-breeding relate to autosomal recessive genes. These are described and discussed in Chapter 3.

Biosocial perspective on the family

The second topic to be addressed in this debate about incest is contemporary views and debate about "the family". The relevant aspects of this are not whether the nuclear family is a thing of the past, or a construct of male oppression of women, but in the wider sense of whatever pattern has been developed in any cultural or racial group for the protection of the young of that group and their childhood rearing. Troost defines it thus:

> *'Family members are related by blood or marriage. They interact in a social arena of co-operation and conflict.'* [8]

The social anthropologist, Strathern, writes with a different emphasis:

> *'Persons related to one another through ties of procreation are specially marked as "kin". Kinship is thus in the West regarded as rooted in biology, but serves in the double biological role of (a) genetic connection and (b) nurture and childrearing.'* *

---

*Anthropologists would also say that in other societies we find similar ranges of persons demarcated by their involvement in procreation and nurture, but those who are defined in this way may include persons whom a westerner would exclude on biological grounds and exclude others a westerner would include.

This is in tune with a sociobiological perspective of "the family". Such a perspective argues the following:

> *'Human families present a unique variation (from the rest of the animal species)...because the scope and depth of their relatedness has been extended through the subsequent development of marriage. That institution reflects the human potential to create bonds and linkages that reach far beyond the immediate confines of genetic linkage...Homo sapiens' ability to originate and maintain lasting intimate relationships, dyadic or otherwise...permitted the development of forms of parenting that distinguish human families from those of other living species.'* [9]

Given this, and the explanations for the origin of the incest taboo and its possible significance for the stability and continuation of a human society, it is understandable that incestuous relationships are viewed with disapproval, outrage and, we would suggest, an element of fear – fear of their potential for destructiveness of how any society functions. They break so many of its perceived basic "rules". But do we all share a horror of incest and experience the strength of the incest taboo in equal measure?

Common understandings

La Fontaine, from a social anthropologist's point of view, writes about contemporary attitudes:

> *'The idea of sexual activity, particularly intercourse, with a child arouses the deepest concern, even outrage, among all but a tiny minority. What most people consider normal sexual activity is in fact shaped by convention and custom, which differ from place to place...In Britain, heterosexual vaginal intercourse is what is thought to be the normal by the majority...'*

Other forms of sexual activity are tolerated but may be seen as 'abnormal' or labelled as deviant or perverted.

> *'Sexual activities with children, however, are almost universally condemned as a violation of what is normal sexual behaviour; the possibility arouses feelings of disgust and horror.'* [10]

It is well known that child molesters have a rough time in prison where they are ostracised and victimised as not part of the group, even by those who have themselves broken the rules of society.

The other side of the argument put forward by a minority is that by repressing children's sexual nature, more harm is done to them than by sexual activities between adults and children. But such views are overwhelmingly disproved by the evidence of the lasting harm done to children in such situations – the invasion of their bodies combined with their position of trapped powerlessness.

The term "incest" is in itself emotive, but considerable confusion has arisen about it and the concept of "taboos" by the previously mentioned tendency of many writers and the media to use the terms incest and child sexual abuse as if interchangeable. This confusion is apparent in social work literature too and so social workers themselves find that their professional and personal ideas can also be confused. However, it is possible to sort out the different levels at which the public and the community we live in react.

La Fontaine's analysis is useful here.

> 'Incest between parents and children is regarded as unthinkable, by which most people mean that it could not, and does not, happen among normal people...Brother/sister (sibling) incest is generally regarded with much less horror than incest between generations. It is widely thought that a certain amount of sexual experimentation may go on between young brothers and sisters. This is seen as childish and shortlived, hardly to be counted as "incest"...In fact, sibling incest may be seen in a rather romantic light; the chance meeting of a brother and sister brought up separately and not knowing each other's identity...more as a tragic love affair than an offence.' [11]

However, reality suggests a different scenario, particularly where there is a difference in age, imposed secrecy and/or bribery or coercion.

Incest involves the breaking of a taboo. There is horror that adults could behave in such a way towards children – their own families; that they could misuse their adult power; that the result is the ensuing breaking of trust that assumes parents will protect their young. The reactions to the findings of the Cleveland Report showed opinions ranging from horrified acceptance that child sexual abuse is of greater magnitude than had been generally realised, to angry disbelief.[12] Whichever is the predominant opinion in any community or group, no one is immune. Individuals and groups can and will respond in different ways.

Issues for social workers and other professionals

Professionals working with such families also react emotionally and are subject to these fears. They have to free themselves from simply reacting in a way dictated by the effects of being acculturised to their cultural group's views and by their own experience of family sexuality. All, too, will be aware from their observation of young children and their own childhood experiences that around the ages of three and four most boys want to marry their mothers and become a daddy and most girls talk of having babies when they grow up and say, 'I'll marry you, Daddy, when I grow up.'

Freud's theorising and writing about this Oedipal phase have been very influential but also controversial. There is a continuing debate about how his original assertion that many female patients being treated for hysteria reported sexual abuse by their fathers was changed by him into a belief that this was fantasy and not reality. The fantasy interpretation became a central theme in his thinking and theorising. Without entering into this controversy which is well-documented elsewhere,[13] the Oedipal stage in normal child development is well-documented and observable in young children.

Children born of incestuous relationships are proof that in many families and adult-child relationships the innocence of the three to four-year-old's fantasy love of a parent of the opposite sex has been translated into reality. Even if we do not believe in witchcraft, omens and revengeful spirits, we all have memories of children's fables and the tragic stories of Oedipus and others in myth and legend to remind us that breaking the basic mores of any society's sexual codes can produce dire consequences where the innocent actors suffer as much as the knowing villains. Many texts provide a full exposition of this.[14]

Add to this the teaching and influence of the different religions and denominations in the Judaic Christian cultures and traditions that sexual relationships outside of marriage are sinful, then those that also break the incest taboo are bound to become even more "sinful" and condemned. In Islamic law there are similar sexual prohibitions, and in Hindu societies, even where marriage between cousins is actually encouraged in some communities to preserve family ties, sexual relationships between close relatives are abhorred.

As well as the multicultural religious aspects there is an additional and particular dilemma for social workers who are seeking to have a balanced view in this area of work. Over several decades there has been an emphasis on environmental factors as having a determining influence on human behaviour. Child care practice and research has given weight and credence to this. In social work education, radical sociology has had a strong impact, emphasising the importance and influence of environment and the structural aspects of our society as determinants of outcome. In the last decade, however, there has been growing recognition of the importance of genetic factors and the input of heredity and predisposition. This has been fuelled by the writings and experience of family psychiatrists and other clinicians and the increasing accuracy of genetic mapping. Interaction between the two has become a prerequisite for a balanced theoretical stance.

Certainly, where children are born as a result of incest, the genetic uncertainties loom large and cannot be ignored. Does the genetic makeup of these children set them apart? Can the usual concepts in social work literature of planning for children be used? Should they be viewed as possibly having disabilities or should the question of incest be ignored? There is a very real risk that in practice they will be viewed as disabled and as having devolopmental problems and therefore "hard-to-place" because of the incest. The case studies indicate some of the possible outcomes for such confusion and fearfulness.

Legal view of incest

What does contemporary UK law say about incest? What is its meaning in criminal law? We have seen that confusion exists both in the literature and the community with regard to concepts about incest. It is interesting to note that this is reflected in the legal statutes relating to incest in different countries. We deal here only with the law in England and Wales and in Scotland, but this is sufficient to illustrate this point, as well as to offer readers information that may be relevant to their work.

In England and Wales, the law on incest falls short of protecting many of the children concerned. It is dealt with in Sections 10 and 11 of the Sexual Offences Act 1956, which reads as follows:

> Section 10(1): It is an offence for a man to have sexual intercourse with a woman whom he knows to be his grand-daughter, daughter, sister or mother.

> Section 11(1): It is an offence for a woman of the age of sixteen or over to permit a man whom she knows to be her grandfather, father, brother or son to have sexual intercourse with her by her consent.

The prohibition applies only to biological relationships in a direct line to the person concerned, with or without marriage. It applies to half-brothers and sisters, but not to uncles and aunts.

Because of the biological factor, sexual intercourse between those related by adoption, therefore, is not prohibited in England and Wales. Section 39 of The Adoption Act 1976 (which deals with the status of adopted children and, among other things, provides that an adopted child shall be treated in law as the child of the adopters and not of anyone else) is specifically excluded from applying to Sections 10 and 11 of the Sexual Offences Act (Section 47(1) of The Adoption Act 1976). So no offence is committed by an adoptive father who has sexual intercourse with his adopted daughter, other than when the offence is indecency or unlawful sexual intercourse with a young person under sixteen years.

The offence of incest is punishable by a maximum of seven years' imprisonment, or life imprisonment in the case of sexual intercourse with a girl under thirteen years.

The Criminal Law Revision Committee in 1980 published a working paper on sexual offences in which it sought views on a recommendation that it should be an offence for a man to have sexual intercourse with his legally adopted daughter under the age of eighteen. Other minor changes to the law were also canvassed, including the desirability of exempting young people under eighteen (rather than sixteen as at present) from criminal liability for consensual intercourse with a grandfather or father. No action has, however, been taken to date on any of these suggestions or recommendations.

Legal prohibitions in Scotland are wider under The Incest and Related Offences (Scotland) Act 1986, Section 1. The table set out in this Act includes not only uncles, aunts, great-grandparents and great-grandsons or daughters, but also adoptive parents and children. The list does not, however, include adoptive siblings.

The Scottish Act adds to the English list of sexual offences against children under sixteen years a new category, that is, sexual intercourse by a person who is "a member of the household of the child" and "is in a position of trust or authority in relation to that child".

Social workers in this field have become aware that the betrayal of trust can be as harmful to the development of an abused child as can the physical act, and it is interesting to note that the more recent Scottish legislation comes closer to recognising this than does the legislation in England and Wales.

Although many cases of incest dealt with by child care workers could involve two criminal offences, that of incest plus an additional sexual offence against children, not all children born as a result of incest will be the result of abuse. Some of them will be born to an adult who has consented to intercourse.

Summary of discussion in this chapter

Incest and child sexual abuse are not synonymous, although the media and many writers often present them as if they were.

The incest taboo has several possible explanations. It seems likely that a mixture of factors should be seen as relevant to understanding the impact of this concept on individuals and groups. Myths and legends have reinforced the prohibition of sexual activities between near relatives. Religious tradition has added to this.

In common understandings of incest, different layers of acceptance or non-acceptance can be identified. Social workers are part of this and have the added dilemma, as far as the children resulting from incest are concerned, of having to resolve the relative emphasis to accord to environment or to heredity and genes. The law defines incest in terms of a criminal act and includes within it different relationships depending on which side of the border between England and Scotland the offence is committed and a resulting child is born.

The child born as a result of consummated heterosexual activity between near relatives or those acting in that role can claim in law to have a mother, but who their father is is open to interpretation because of dual relationship roles. Many such children are brought up within their families of origin with their true status shrouded in secrecy. Those who are not may be totally rejected by their families of origin. Such are the group who are most likely to be referred to social work agencies. The families are often secretive about their true origins. To be open involves the law and possible criminal proceedings against a family member. Keeping the secret or not then becomes someone else's responsibility.

But whose secret is it really? Should it stay a secret? Has it any relevance for the child thus conceived? The next chapter addresses these questions.

References

1 La Fontaine, J, *Child Sexual Abuse*, Polity Press, pp 23 & 24, 1990.

2 Pasternak, B, *Introduction to Kinship and Social Organisation*, Prentice Hall, p 29, 1976.

3 See 2 above, p 31.

4 Quoted by Turvill, P, in 'Incest', *Adoption & Fostering*, Vol 104(2), 1981.

5 See 2 above, p 36.

6 See 2 above, pp 37-41.

7 For example, (a) Reynolds, V, and Kellett, J, eds, *Mating and Marriage*, Biosocial Society Series 3, Oxford University Press, 1991 and (b) Fox, R, *The Red Lamp of Incest*, University of Notre Dame Press, 1980, USA.

8 Troost, K M, in ed Filsinger, E E, *Biosocial Perspectives on the Family*, Sage, p 188, 1988.

9 Sprey, J, in ed Filsinger, E E, *Biosocial Perspectives on the Family*, Sage, pp 145 & 146, 1988.

10 See 1 above, p 21.

11 See 1 above, p 27.

12 Butler-Sloss, Lord Justice E, *Report by the Inquiry into Child Abuse in Cleveland*, HMSO, p 11, para 36, 1987.

13 For example, (a) Wasserman, S and Rosenfeld, A, An Overview of the History of Child Sexual Abuse and Sigmund Freud's Contributions in eds, O'Donohue, W, and Geer, J H, *The Sexual Abuse of Children: Theory and Research*, Vol 1, 1992, USA, Lawrence Erlbaum Associates, and (b) Masson, J, *The Assault on Truth: Freud and Child Sexual Abuse*, (Harper Collins Edition) Fontana, 1992.

14 For example, (a) Wasserman, S and Rosenfeld, A, *op cit*, Ch 4 and (b) Rush, F, *The Best-kept Secret: Sexual Abuse of Children*, McGraw-Hill, 1980.

2 Children's need for genealogical knowledge

Family secrets

The numbers of children born as a result of incestuous relationships is unknown. They are submerged in a sea of silence. No references about them are available in a literature search of UK and North American sources other than regarding genetic issues. A brief reference from New Zealand is quoted in Chapter 9. Brinich, writing in the USA in *Adoption from the Inside* gave as evidence some detail about the psychiatric treatment of one mother who had given birth to such a child.[1] However, he commented further:

> *'The reality that some adopted children are the products of incestuous unions is undeniable. I would even venture to say that many more adoptees are incestuous in origin than we will ever know, as this kind of situation is easily hidden, and hidden with the full weight of our cultural taboo against incest.'*

Until recently, the whole area of child sexual abuse was, of course, shrouded in secrecy and this makes us want to believe there are not many such children. With the lifting of the veil to reveal the true extent of child sexual abuse, both numerically and within all social and economic classes, there may well now be uncovered a whole group of children whose origins were previously unknown. All those working with birth mothers placing their babies for adoption will now become more aware of the possibility that the pregnancy is from an incestuous relationship, particularly where the mother is very young.

This chapter will deal with family secrets and who does or should tell any child about their origins. This task is something many adults, for their own adult reasons, find difficult to undertake, or choose to avoid. It is not surprising that those who are born as a result of incest are not told about their origins and that there remains a continuing reluctance to address the issue, given the existence of a long-standing and deep-seated taboo surrounding it. However, these children are the visible proof that the taboo has been broken. They are the visible reminders of a union forbidden by society.

In fact, some might say, why tell them? Why should we impose on them the burden of knowledge they do not need to have? As a foster carer in one of our cases believed: 'Perhaps he should never be told. Doesn't he have enough to cope with?' Social workers also have strong emotions and feelings and have experienced their culture's view of incest. Why should they take the responsibility of foisting on these children what they perceive to be a burden they can never throw off? If the children know, will life be better for them or worse?

Evidence from studies regarding the need for information

The knowledge that adopted children need to know about their birth families was originally obtained from several research studies[2,3,4] and confirmed in clinical studies.[5]

These studies, particularly McWhinnie's study, *Adopted Children: How they grow up*,[6] addressed for the first time the question of how adopted children experience their upbringing and who they perceive as their parents. This study was based on retrospective interviews with a representative group of adopted adults living in the community; it was neither a follow-up from an agency group nor a clinic population nor a study of adoption as seen from the perspective of the adoptive parents. It showed how the children's identification and loyalty was to their nurturing psychological parents but that they needed information about those to whom they were born and why they were placed for adoption, or rather why they were not kept by their birth family.

Other studies which also considered the child's perspective, and conducted in the UK, South Africa and Germany, confirmed the earlier work.[7,8,9] Triseliotis' study of those who took their curiosity to the point of obtaining their original birth certificate (as has always been possible in Scotland since adoption was made legal in 1930) further confirmed that active curiosity about origins was not necessarily a sign of rejection of the adoptive family. His study showed, however, that searching was done by the least well-adjusted adopted adults.[10] Since then, other studies show that it requires considerable courage to initiate this step of searching.[11,12,13] This is significant for understanding adopted adults' views and echoed findings from the earlier studies as well.

Contemporary data is now emerging about those in the UK who actually search and why,[14,15] and about reunions, but much less exists about those who do not, so such studies always have a specific population bias towards the two out of five adopted adults who are likely to search. However, the cumulative evidence over the various studies and over many years is overwhelming in its main drift.

In the UK, therefore, there is now a general acceptance and understanding that adopted children should be told of their adoption and be given information about their birth families.* What is not so generally recognised is that this is not accepted in many other countries. For example, in the USA and Canada the adoption legislation in many states and provinces respectively forbids access to such information. Nor is it always recognised that for adopters and carers sharing information of this kind is not always easy to achieve, even where legislative provision is favourable to it.

The situation about needing to know their own early history is similar for foster children and it is surprising that this has not been recognised sooner for they too experience separation from and loss of contact with their birth family. There has been no protective legislation for them in this respect and case files of children in care were often destroyed systematically when the children were deemed to have reached adult status.

Now, at last, that has been remedied. The Children Act 1989 in England and Wales recognises the need for children in public care to have some form of continuing links with birth families. The Foster Placement (Children's) Regulations 1991 following on that Act, stipulate that children's records must be preserved for 75 years. Research studies too have shown that foster children, like adopted children, need to have information and certainty about their birth families.[16]

With the increase in family break-downs and divorce, there is a

---

*The DoH Review of Adoption Law: Report to Ministers of an Interdepartmental Group: A Consultation Document 1992 paras 4.1–5.8 recognises this. It is hoped and assumed that Scotland will develop a similar emphasis in impending legislation.

growing group of children who are separated from continual contact with one of their birth parents. If their need for knowledge about the non-custodial parent and that part of their family is not acknowledged either by continuing contact or letters or family discussions, then information about their earlier life may never be shared. They too will then have a void in their genealogical history.

Children's comprehension of information about origins

The research findings that are particularly relevant for the present discussion are those about the psychology of adoptive family relationships and communication. These have recently been summarised by Hoopes in *The Psychology of Adoption*.[17] This shows the complexity of how adults and children can or cannot share sensitive details about the children's origins. Perhaps most telling is the evidence about adult assumptions.

> *'Children cannot understand certain situations, that they should not be given answers to some of their questions since in this way they will forget about the wonderings which give rise to their questions, and also that children do not hear the comments of adults (if the children are playing or reading) and observe happenings between adults.'* [18]

In fact, children are very sensitive to these and quickly absorb messages that there is something "different" about them that people avoid talking about. In this way, many have suspected that they are adopted long before they are told. A source of great resentment to adopted children is where something is known or hinted at as being general family knowledge about them but is never referred to openly.[19]

The one-way communication about adoption is documented but not always recognised, that is, the child expects the adults in his or her life to take the initiative and tell them about their origins. What is less well acknowledged, however, are the subtleties of such communication.

> *'The child...though wanting to be given information about why and how their adoption was arranged could not ask...Even when the subject was raised on the initiative of adoptive parents, the child frequently feigned indifference.'* [20]

This kind of stalemate is quite unnerving for adoptive parents and for anyone involved in sharing crucial information with children. When the information is about incest, great sensitivity is needed to understand what the feigned indifference really means. The case histories discussed later in this study give examples of this apparent indifference.

The fact that many adopted children report that they will only seek their birth parent after the death of their adoptive parents is again clear evidence that children do not question the reticence of their carers to an extent that still surprises many, yet, in fact, many adoptive parents expect them to ask questions. The children also feel loyalty to those who have cared for them. This is confirmed within the study, *Access to Birth Records*,[21] and the contemporary experience of those who seek help from the post-adoption centres. There are two examples of this in the histories discussed later.

Although so far we have referred to "telling" as if it were a one-off event, this is inaccurate on two counts: first, the other side of the "telling" act is, of course, the understanding by the child of the content of the telling; and secondly, that the process has to be viewed as one spanning a period of time. Disclosure over time is a much more relevant concept than telling. Brodzinsky's work has been very illuminating here.[22] While the original studies of adoptive family functioning revealed that children want open discussion of adoption within the immediate family, they do not wish constant reference to it to outsiders. They are the son or daughter of the parents – not the adopted son or adopted daughter. Also, too frequent references to the birth family become disturbing: 'It is like planting a tree but digging up the roots frequently to see if it has taken root.'[23]

What Brodzinsky has done is to provide specific data about what understanding children actually have about "adoption" and family relationships at different ages. At the ages of four or five, children hear and accept the word "adopted" but not all of them understand the significance or the difference between adoption and birth. In Brodzinsky's research, 45 per cent understood the difference. At this age all of them were excited about the concept of being different and special. At the ages of eight or nine, about 50 per cent appreciated the difference; of the 50 per cent who did not, half questioned whether the placement was permanent. Brodzinsky argues first, that because children have been told it does not mean they understand, and second, that the limitations of understanding are not necessarily a product of how the telling is done but result from the limitations of the child's cognitive understanding. Hence his emphasis on "disclosure over time".

The evidence from adoption studies shows the ages of eight or nine to be the critical time for discussion of parent figures and a time when many adopted children experience comments from their peers which are not phrased in the most complimentary terms. It is, for example, a time of increased referrals of adopted children to child psychiatric clinics and an age when children's conceptual understanding of death changes from a simplistic matter-of-fact acceptance to a realisation of the loss of personal relationships that death involves.

By puberty and adolescence, adopted, fostered and stepchildren are asking – as are the majority of their peers – who am I? Those in this present study also show evidence of this questioning for information about themselves, uncertainty about their own identity and puzzlement about why they were cared for outside of their birth families.

Social workers in the UK need to understand and appreciate the concept of "disclosure over time" and its complexities. The emphasis in social work literature so far, however, has been on the "how" of telling, the techniques to use, etc. What also needs to be addressed is the stage of cognitive, social and emotional development of the child[24] and the fact that there may not be congruence between these different aspects. An awareness of these aspects is as important as the relationship and emotional climate in which the child is living.

Features of all of these emerge as very significant in the case studies quoted later and are relevant to the question of when to tell about the incest. In addition, it has to be borne in mind that different methods of sharing information with children have to be appropriate to their age. Drawings and puppets for younger children, life story books with photographs, visits to where they used to live, etc, and games and genograms for others, are essential to replace or supplement verbal communication.

What information do the children need?
To those without it, information about origins means details of who they were born to and why their first mother (and father) did not keep them. A specific area highlighted in much adoption research is the need for

those separated from their birth family to have accurate and detailed information about their biological family's health record. For example, the question at a hospital attendance, "Is there any history of this in your family?" calls for a factual reply if the person concerned is to maintain a sense of certainty about self. It is a potent issue for children of incest and is raised vividly in one of our case studies in which detailed medical information proved to be very reassuring. Uncertainty about who you are and who your forebears may have been is a constant, negative theme in all the in-depth research studies and in counselling and clinical practice. Any factual reality is seen as preferable. Again, this is illustrated in the case examples discussed in later chapters.

The attitudes of adults involved

That children can take on board as personal to themselves adults' critical attitudes about their birth family is not surprising. Those working on placement plans for children in all forms of substitute care should therefore always explore with potential carers their attitudes to particular scenarios about the background and family of origin of the children they may be caring for.

And what of the wider family of the substitute carers – how important are they and their attitudes? The early adoption studies referred to previously in this chapter showed vividly that the wider kinship group can often undo the caring atmosphere of the more intimate nuclear family, a finding reinforced from post-adoption counselling experience.[25]

The placement situation for the children of this study is then a potential minefield of adult prejudices and fears. Social workers will try to discuss the issues in advance with potential carers and their relations. We were presented with information from a medical adviser to an agency* which showed that although adopters were thus prepared and were open and accepting about the facts of the children's origins in the children's early years, the development of their sexuality as they reached puberty and adolescence revealed cracks in how accepting the carers really had been.

---

*The medical advisor was a member of the working group which collected case studies for this project. She was responding to telephone calls she had received during the course of her work.

They were afraid of "history repeating itself" and found themselves distrustful of the adoptive brother and adoptive sister's physical proximity in quite harmless daily living, or suspicious of a potential relationship between the spouse of the opposite sex and the child. The adoptive parents hated themselves for these unwelcome thoughts, and found their family relationships were in jeopardy as a consequence.

So it really is tempting not to share information about incest with carers and to ask the question, "Is it really necessary to tell the children?" If they don't know, they will never suspect and you can then shield them from what you, as an adult, see as unpleasant facts. But the research studies have shown that they will suspect that there is something there. Our case examples show this awareness and puzzlement. They also show children's resilience to knowing and accepting the truth. This is in line with the writing of Winnicott[26] and others subsequently, that children can accept the most horrendous scenarios if these are explained in a way sensitive to the child's point of view and appropriate to their level of understanding.

References

1 Brinich, P M, Adoption from the Inside Out, in ed Brodzinsky, D M, and Schechter, M D, *The Psychology of Adoption*, Oxford University Press, pp 59-60, 1990.

2 Kornitzer, M, *Adoption and Family Life*, Putnam, 1968.

3 McWhinnie, A M, *Adopted Children: How they grow up*, Routledge & Kegan Paul, 1967.

4 Raynor, L, *The Adopted Child Comes of Age*, Allen & Unwin, 1980.

5 Sants, H J 'Genealogical Bewilderment in Children with Substitute Parents' in *British Journal of Medical Psychology* No 37, 1964.

6 See 3 above.

7 See 4 above.

8 Boult, B E, *Salient Experiences of a Sample of Adult Adoptees*, Dissertation for MA, University of Cape Town (unpublished), South Africa, 1987.

9 Ebertz, B, *Adoption als Identitätsproblem*, Lambertus, Freiburg im Breisgau, Germany, 1987.

10 Triseliotis, J, *In Search of Origins*, Routledge & Kegan Paul, 1973.

11 Erlich, H, *A Time to Search: The moving and dramatic stories of adoptees in search of their natural parents*, Paddington Press Ltd, 1977, USA.

12 Toynbee, P, *Lost Children: The story of adopted children looking for their mothers*, Hutchinson, 1985.

13 Walby, C M and Symons, B, *Who Am I? Identity, adoption and human fertilisation*, 1990.

14 Haimes, E, and Timms, N, *Adoption, Identity and Social Policy: The search for distant relatives*, Gower, 1985.

15 (a) Day, C, et al, 'Access to Birth Records: General Register Office Study', *Adoption & Fostering* Vol 98(4), pp 17-28, 1979 and (b) Hall, T, ed, *Access to Birth Records: The impact of section 26 of the Children Act, 1975*, Day, C and Leeding, H, BAAF, 1980.

16 Rowe, J, et al, *Long-term Foster Care*, Batsford, 1984.

17 Hoopes, J L, 'Adoption and Identity Formation', in ed Brodzinsky D M, and Schechter M D, p 165-166, *The Psychology of Adoption*, Oxford University Press, 1990.

18 See 3 above p 265.

19 See 3 above p 265.

20 See 3 above p 248.

21 See 15 b) above pp 20 and 32.

22 Brodzinsky, D M, et al (1984) 'Children's Understanding of Adoption' in *Child Development* No 55, pp 869-878, 1984.

23 See 3 above,.

24 Erikson, E, (1950, 1963), *Childhood and Society*, republished by Paladin, Collins, 1977, USA and *The Life Cycle Completed: A Review*, Norton, 1982, USA.

25 McWhinnie, A M, 'Group Counselling with 78 Adoptive Families' in Tod, R, ed, *Social Work in Adoption*, Longman, 1971.

26 Winnicott, D M, (a) *The Child, the Family and the Outside World*, Penguin, 1973 and Penguin, 1991 and (b) *Playing and Reality*, Tavistock, 1971.

3   The genetic facts and their disclosure

Professor J A Raeburn

Chapter 1 described some of the religious and cultural traditions which have deep-seated taboos against incestuous relationships, as well as severe legal strictures. It could be argued that these are based on empirical observations made centuries ago. Even in the absence of an understanding of genetic principles, it could have been noted then that there were greater risks of disabilities in the offspring of such matings. Here, we describe the genetic situations which can result from incest and how these may be recognised in individual families. We suggest that genetic counselling experience of how to disclose disturbing genetic information can provide appropriate guidelines for tackling discussion of incest in specific family situations. To understand the subject an initial brief knowledge of modern genetics is essential.

Genetic principles

Genetic disorders are classified into four main groups, each of which provides a logical model to investigate and a mechanism to explain the features of a family tree (Table 1). Single gene disorders are further sub-divided into dominants and recessives. They are due to changes (mutations) which occur in specific genes. These can be located either on the non-sex chromosomes (that is, the autosomes) or on the X chromosome (or, very rarely, the Y chromosome). For a brief summary of the principles of inheritance the reader is referred to Connor and Ferguson-Smith.[1]

To understand *single gene conditions* it should be appreciated that most genes are paired, each member of a pair being inherited from one or other parent. Therefore a given genetic condition, which is determined by a gene in a specific genetic position (locus) on an autosome, the features in the individual person will depend on the interplay of the abnormal and normal genes. If one gene of the pair dominates, it is referred to as an *autosomal dominant characteristic.*

Table 1

Four categories of genetic disorder

Single gene disorders
Chromosome disorders
Multifactorial disorders
Somatic cell genetic disorders

Many diseases are due to autosomal dominant genes (eg., Huntington's Disease, Marfan's syndrome or polycystic kidney disease). Usually the family tree of a dominant disease will show affected people in each generation. The affected person will have inherited the disorder from one or other parent. If a parent has a dominant condition, and therefore shows features of the genetic disease, the offspring have a 50 per cent chance of inheriting the abnormal gene. The converse of autosomal dominant disorders are *autosomal recessive disorders*. These are of great importance in considering the genetic problems of incestuous relationships and will be covered in detail later.

Chromosomal disorders involve not just single functioning genes but often large groups, which are in particular positions on chromosomes. One can imagine a chromosome as resembling a long open bead necklace in which individual beads represent individual genes. Disorders of chromosomes are due to either duplications/deletions (when a particular chromosome segment is duplicated or deleted) or changes in number (an extra chromosome or a missing one).

Polygenic disorders involve the combined interplay of several different genes which could be located in different chromosomal locations. Polygenic disorders are also usually influenced by factors in the environment such as toxic chemicals or dietary deficiencies. They are then known as *multifactorial disorders*. For example, spina bifida is a multifactorial disorder, being due to both genetic factors and environmental changes. The environmental element probably involves a relative deficiency of folic acid in the maternal diet in the early stages of pregnancy.

Somatic cell disorders are genetic changes (mutations) which occur in cells of specific parts of the body (lung, breast, gut, eye, etc.), to cause diseases such as cancer. They tend to occur by conferring a susceptibility to disease, not a specific high risk. Although cancer is known to have a genetic basis, for practical purposes the children of incest are not likely to have an increased susceptibility to it. There is no evidence that a child of incest is more likely to be affected by somatic cell genetic disorders but this is an area which needs further investigation.

Although chromosomal and somatic cell disorders could occur in children of incest, they would be no more likely to do so than in children of unrelated matings. The genetic problems most likely in children of incestuous matings are those due to *autosomal recessiveness* and therefore a more detailed description of the basis of this type of inheritance follows. Other single gene disorders may occur in families in which incest has occurred, but except in the rare situation of both of the incest partners being affected by the same dominant gene, the child of incest would be at no more risk of a dominant than other children. In such rare situations and also when a sex-linked disorder (i.e. one due to an abnormality on the X chromosome) is present, referral to a geneticist is essential.

Autosomal recessive inheritance

As described above, autosomal single gene disorders occur when either one or both members of a particular gene pair is abnormal. The abnormal member of the gene pair could have been inherited from either parent. Dominant disorders have already been described, the gene being expressed when, in a single dose, it comes from one parent only. In recessive disorders the opposite is the case. For the disorder to occur the person must have a double dose of a recessive gene, the abnormal mutated genes coming from both parents. Consideration of the pattern of affected people in the family often helps to distinguish dominant from recessive disorders. Thus in dominant inheritance, the family tree will include affected people in several generations. Conversely if a person has a recessive disorder they must have inherited one abnormal copy from each parent to give them a double dose of the disease gene. With recessives, it is unusual to have affected people in more than one generation, or even outwith a particular sibship.

Healthy people are carriers of autosomal recessive disorders without being in any way abnormal. It has been calculated that on average everyone carries two or three recessive genes,[2] which in double dose would be lethal.

Carriers have a single copy of the abnormal recessive gene (plus one copy of the normal one), whilst affected people have two copies, one inherited from each parent. In any family, close relatives are more likely to be carriers of the same recessive gene. Thus in incestuous relationships both partners are more likely to be carriers and the offspring has an increased chance of a double dose. If a known autosomal recessive condition already exists in a family, then the risk to children of incest is higher.

The relevance of autosomal recessiveness to children of incest
Children of incest may have autosomal recessive conditions which are much less likely in the offspring of normal people. Figure 1 illustrates autosomal recessive inheritance. Because this is the most important form of inheritance in the offspring of incestuous matings, it is useful to consider this model of inheritance carefully. The concept is best understood if one thinks about the intermediate stage between parents (I.1 and I.2) who are carriers of an abnormal gene (their genetic type is indicated in the figure as NA), and their affected child (II.2), who has a double dose of the abnormal gene and is therefore AA. The intermediate stage is the formation of eggs and sperms in the mother and father respectively. In both eggs and sperms the chromosome number is halved compared to all other body cells, there being one and not two copies of

Figure 1
Autosomal recessive inheritance

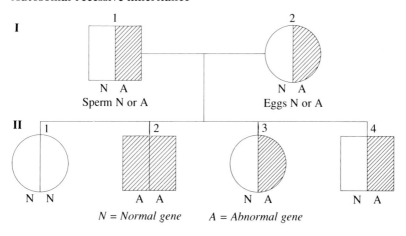

N = Normal gene A = Abnormal gene

each chromosome (and hence one copy only of each gene). Thus, in our example, the individual egg or sperm will have either the normal gene (N) or the abnormal one (A).

The nature of autosomal recessive diseases

Autosomal recessive conditions are very varied and can cause physical or mental disabilities, or both. The specific diagnosis may depend on the pattern of abnormalities present. Six hundred and thirty one autosomal recessive diseases are recognised.[3] Commonly, autosomal recessive disorders are severe and have an early age of onset, often involving diagnostic features at birth. Table 2 gives the commonest examples of autosomal recessive disorders, all of which tend to have differing frequencies in different populations. Affected people may die in childhood but, for many conditions, there has been a steady slow improvement in the prognosis. Since most autosomal recessives cause severe disease their presence in a child of incest would usually be obvious. However, provided this can be carried out without causing extra emotional trauma to the individual teenager, examination by an experienced paediatrician or geneticist should be considered in late childhood to exclude the possibility of disorder. Children of incest who are examined during adolescence will either have obvious autosomal recessive disease or could be assumed to have escaped these conditions, probably being completely normal. This fact is important because although children of incest will have been at quite high genetic risk at conception, if they are normal in childhood then they are unlikely to develop problems later. Assuming they do not have consanguineous matings themselves, their own children are not at increased genetic risk.

Table 2

Autosomal recessive conditions

DISEASE	POPULATION WITH HIGHEST FREQUENCY
Cystic fibrosis	White Europeans
Sickle cell anaemia	African-Caribbeans
Tay-Sachs disease	Ashkenazi Jews
Thalassaemia	Mediterranean populations (eg, Cypriots)

Genetic risks of incest

Although there have been few studies of the genetic consequences of incestuous matings it is clear that the high risk of abnormality predicted theoretically is borne out in practice. Seemanova compared a group of 161 children of incestuous matings with 95 of their half-siblings and showed that the children of incest had significantly increased infant mortality, congenital malformation and a lower intelligence level than their half-siblings who had unrelated parents.[4] In a later follow-up of this work in which the two groups were better matched and had more intensive study, she confirmed the earlier findings and showed that the incest group had a lower birth weight and higher mortality than their half-siblings.[5] In total, 38 per cent of the incest group and 4.1 per cent of the controls had significant genetic defects. Adams and Neel found that only seven of 18 children of incestuous unions were normal.[6] Bundey reviewed these and other studies and concluded that in children of father/daughter or brother/sister unions less than half were normal, one quarter were severely mentally disabled and a further third were mildly retarded.[7] Recognisable autosomal recessives occurred in 14 per cent and congenital malformations (usually multifactorial) in 12 per cent. There is some evidence for a significant but slight increase in the frequency of multifactorial disorders in the offspring of consanguineous, especially incestuous, matings.[8]

Termination of pregnancy

Because of the increased risk of abnormality in the offspring, pregnancies resulting from incestuous relationships may often be considered for termination. This decision would lie primarily with the pregnant woman, but on genetic grounds such a decision could be supported. It must be appreciated that a termination in this circumstance would add a further probable cause for guilt in the woman who has been the victim of an incestuous relationship. There is a great need for counselling support, and this may continue for many years after the event. The latest genetic investigations, including ultrasound investigations in the pregnancy, may either reassure that the baby is as normal as can be determined or give clear evidence of serious abnormality, and thus clarify the justification for abortion on medical grounds, if, after counselling, the mother requests it.

Incest and mental disability

Recently Jancar and Johnston reviewed the literature on the frequency of mental disability in the offspring of incestuous relationships and reported their own retrospective study.[9] Using records of 1000 inpatients at hospitals for mental illness in Bristol, they identified 11 incestuous unions which had produced a total of 38 offspring. Twenty five of those were mentally disabled; a further five died in infancy. Only 5/38 were confirmed as normal. In the incestuous unions, five were brother/sister matings, five were father/daughter and one uncle/niece. In these 11 unions, eight of the mothers were reported to have below normal intelligence. With the small numbers it was not possible to compare the risk of mental disability (or of any genetic disorder) in the three different types of incestuous union.

Disclosure of information about incest

Because of the strong feelings caused by the knowledge that incest has occurred, disclosure of this information must be carried out with extreme sensitivity and care. Who has the right to know? Table 3 lists those other than the incest partners who should be offered genetic information and counselling support.

Table 3

Who needs to know?

Offspring of incestuous matings
Adoptive parents
Family doctor of child of incest (certain medical specialists)
Key social worker

The attitude of professionals to incest is a further factor to be considered. In a study of 299 health professionals in the USA, Eisenberg et al showed that health visitors, medical students or nursing staff at a hospital for mentally disabled offenders had differing perceptions of the seriousness of incest in terms of harm caused to the abused child. For example, father/daughter incest was regarded as more severe than brother/sister.

The perception by professionals of the nature of incest will influence their ability and inclination to disclose to adoptive parents or the offspring of incest. The case histories in the following chapters give considerable information about the person disclosing as well as about the reactions of the offspring of incest.

A genetic model for disclosure

Occasionally, medical geneticists have to provide sensitive and frightening information to individuals and their families. It could concern a person being at high risk of developing a serious disease, or it could be about the risk of abnormalities in their own offspring. In only the former situation are the children of incest in a different situation from anyone else in the population, unless they mate consanguineously. The closest analogy in the genetic model would be the need to inform young people in a Huntington's Disease family that they might, later on, develop that serious neurological condition.

Disclosure to children of incest

The genetic approach is to discuss fully with the (adoptive) parent(s) or carers and reach agreement about when and how to disclose. Normally a child would not be told about adult onset conditions until they have shown a degree of maturity, roughly equivalent to their sexual development. Thus at 15 or 16 years of age the young person may be told of their risk (eg. 50 per cent) of developing a disorder. For diseases like Huntington's Disease, actual confirmatory pre-symptomatic tests would not be carried out before the age of 18 (International Agreement 1989).[11] There is a generally accepted practice not to perform genetic tests on children who have not received (or understood) the option of deciding whether they wish to be tested.

The above genetic approach could be a starting point for studies of the appropriate mode of disclosure to the children of incest. Many children of incest will be mentally disabled and for them the decision about disclosure of genetic factors must be taken even more sensitively. In some it may be inappropriate and unnecessary. The social and genetic information should be regarded as separate factors. Some children of incest may be affected physically by autosomal recessive conditions such as cystic fibrosis but without having any degree of mental disability.

Disclosure regarding the medical factors should always involve the family doctor, geneticist or physician/paediatrician. That medical person should also ensure that the carer and/or social worker or other trusted person involved is kept in the picture. If children of incest are developing normally, although their family origins could be medically important later in life, there is no genetic risk to offspring unless they mate consanguineously. Therefore the need to disclose and timing will be based on the psychological/emotional elements and will be guided by the carer. I would suggest that the 'cover story'* be planned and discussed with the adoptive parents early in the child's life and that it is based entirely on the facts, not on untruths. As the child asks, the information can be revealed. Adults need to be reminded that young children ask matter of fact questions and usually do not require (or wish) detailed answers. Thus a query about a real mummy or daddy may be simply to find out if they exist. The question has probably no ulterior motive to find out if they are bad. Gradually the development of the cover story, accompanied by straight answers to questions, will lead to full disclosure. Although genetic counselling is not then strictly necessary, it could be offered as reassurance regarding the lack of any genetic problem in the young person's offspring. The author's experience is that most adopted people carry some feelings of guilt and anxiety which trouble them particularly when they plan their own families. The need for reassurance is the major indication for genetic counselling in the teenage child of incest.

Illustrative case studies
The following two case studies are imaginary but include common questions and descriptions of the feelings of several actual people in genetic counselling situations.

Father-daughter incest
A woman who was adopted as a baby discovered when she was in her thirties that her natural mother had a muscle problem which was progressive. She was aware of the strong feelings of guilt in her mother

---

* 'Cover stories' are agreed versions of a child's history so that he or she has an answer for questions asked. They are used in some of the case studies discussed in Part II.

when she met her first at age 20 and at that time also saw her maternal grandfather. There was little contact with her birth family thereafter, even when she married at age 24. She had twin daughters born two years later and coped well with her responsibilities as a mother. When one twin developed a mild muscle problem in the wrist at the age of 16, the woman's anxiety became overwhelming and she was guilt-ridden. Relations with her husband and daughters deteriorated and inpatient psychiatric care and counselling appeared to be of little help. Her birth mother then died and this increased her guilt. Genetic counselling both with a medical geneticist and, at length on many occasions, with a trained genetic nurse specialist, concentrated on the lack of a link between her mother's condition and that of her daughter. Eventually, specialised genetic studies were able to show that the twin daughters had inherited a different chromosome from the grandmother than the one concerned in the latter's muscle disease. There was almost immediate alleviation of the mother's symptoms of anxiety and depression.

In this situation the twins' mother had been a child of incest who was given no information, but whose overtures to her birth mother (and to her father/grandfather) were repelled, presumably because of the family guilt. A more helpful situation would have been for the adoptive parents to have been told about the baby's origins, and in due course about the muscle disease in the birth mother. There was a risk of the twins' mother contracting this condition, but as shown later she did not inherit the abnormal gene; nor did her daughters. Timely disclosure when the woman was reaching adult life could have explained why the incest situation arose and that no evidence was present of any consequent problem in the woman herself. Although the muscle disease in the twin was inevitably going to be a major source of anxiety until it was adequately diagnosed and treated, genetic information about what it was *not* would have given reassurance prior to the woman's severe reactive psychiatric illness.

Brother-sister incest
In this family, there had been a daughter who died at age 16 of cystic fibrosis. All of the energies of both parents had been directed to improving the quality of that girl's life, to the exclusion of all others in the family, particularly the elder brother and younger sister of the affected daughter.

When their sister died, the remaining siblings were aged 18 and 15 respectively and were frequently left entirely on their own. Sexual intercourse took place many times before the girl became pregnant at age 16. The genetic risk to the foetus was high (a one in nine risk of cystic fibrosis) in addition to the theoretical risk of other disabilities. After genetic counselling involving the whole family, and including detailed family therapy from a psychologist, the pregnancy was tested for cystic fibrosis in the baby and screened non-specifically for other disabilities. The results were normal. The baby, healthy at birth (and subsequently shown to be in excellent health throughout childhood) was looked after by the grandparents. She remained in close contact with her birth parents, who continued into higher education. The 'cover story' here was true, that with grandfather and grandmother being so devastated by the illness and death of the first daughter, they did not show their love for the other children, who found that in each other. Long-term supportive counselling was offered in this situation but the family felt that their new orientation was a healthy one and they kept professionals informed without needing further intervention.

These case histories illustrate the entanglement of genetic and emotional issues in many families and the importance of accurate knowledge so that myths are revealed as such, and decisions are made on the basis of the facts.

References

1 Connor, J M, and Ferguson-Smith, M A, *Essential Medical Genetics*, 3rd edition, Blackwell, 1989.

2 Cavalli-Sforza, L L, and Bodmer, W S, *The Genetics of Human Populations*, W H Freeman, 1980, USA.

3 McKusick V A, *Mendelian Inheritance in Man*, 8th edition, Johns Hopkins University Press, 1980, USA.

4 Seemanova, E, 'The Children of Incestuous Matings', *Human Heredity* 21: 108-128, 1971.

5 Seemanova, E, *Genetische Risiko fur Kinder aus Inzest und Verwandtenver-bindungen*, Zeitung Arztliche Fortbildung, 80, 799-802, 1986, Germany.

6 Adams, M S, Neel, J V, 'Children of Incest', *Pediatrics*, 40:55-62, 1967, USA.

7 Bundey S, 'The Child of an Incestuous Union', *Clin Develop. Med.* 74:36-41., 1979.

8 Young, I D, *Introduction to Risk Calculation in Genetic Counselling*, pp 97-103, Oxford Medical Publications, 1991.

9 Jancar, J, and Johnston, S J, 'Incest and Mental Handicap', *J Mental Def. Res.* 34, 483-490, 1990.

10 Eisenberg N, Glynn Owens R, and Dewey M E, 'Attitudes of health professionals to child sexual abuse and incest', *Child Abuse and Neglect*, 11, 109-116, 1987.

11 Harper, P S, Morris, M J, Tyler, A, 'Genetic testing for Huntington's Disease', *British Medical Journal* 300: 1089-1990, 1990.

12 Went L, 'Ethical issues policy statement on Huntington's Disease molecular genetics predictive test', *J Med Genet* 27: 34-38, 1990.

4 The study: how it began and developed

There is general acknowledgement in the UK that when children are adopted they should be told of this. The research studies underpinning this have been described in Chapter 2. The need for adopted children to have access to information and knowledge about their family of origin is acknowledged in contemporary statute,[1] and it is likely to be strengthened in future.

Social work practice over many years has recognised that adopted children should be told of their origins. However, several questions remain: are there situations where adults will deem it unwise or unnecessary to tell children about the circumstances of their conception, or some aspects of their birth family's history? Do you tell a child that his or her father murdered their mother or vice versa? Into this category of facts too dire to tell a child falls the information that they themselves are the result of incestuous relationships. At meetings of child care professionals the answer to the question: 'Would you tell such a child, and if so how would you do it?' the honest answer has always had to be 'we don't know'.

There has also always been the question of how to explain such a background to possible carers and adopters. How could we know if they fully understood and accepted the child and would continue to do so in the future? And what of the genetic risks? How can they be assessed and how can these be shared appropriately with carers and also provide information for the particular children involved?

Many instances in which agencies shied away from placing children born of incestuous relationships have become known to us. There were seen to be too many risks and uncertainties; or perhaps there were unresolved fears of the impact of the incest taboo. Some children may have been aborted unnecessarily out of fear of deformity as well as of social stigma. There are so many layers to these questions that sometimes it seemed simpler to plead ignorance and leave them unanswered. But that, of course, left the problem unsolved.

An opportunity came to address this issue in a systematic way when one of the authors was a member of the Executive Committee of the Medical Group at BAAF. A social worker had asked BAAF for help and support in explaining about origins to a child born of an incestuous union. She wanted useful reading material and to be put in touch with other workers in a similar situation. There was no reservoir of such resources available at BAAF or elsewhere. We decided at last to address the issue with the agreed support of the Medical Group. We knew that details of such children would be recorded in agencies' social work files, even though the numbers known to each agency might be few. Through BAAF's journal, *Adoption & Fostering*, we decided to invite social workers with appropriate experience to get in touch with us. Replies poured in from workers with 'victims' of incestuous abuse, but among these only five social workers, one of them an adoptive parent, had actually worked with children in helping them to understand their origins. This demonstrated at an early stage that the problems of the abused are often confused, and certainly closely associated in the minds of workers, with the problems of children born as a result of the abuse. From this nucleus of five social workers representing six young people, a working party was formed. Also included were a psychiatrist, a medical adviser and a counsellor from an incest helpline who had herself experienced in-family abuse. She was able to provide a personal view of what life is really like in such a family and to show how relationships become distorted thereby creating a web from which it is difficult to escape.

During the course of four meetings, the working party was able to study the six known cases in some depth, and also to learn something about the experiences of other adoptive parents who corresponded with us. Although many issues emerged, some of them common to all the cases, we decided to extend our sample to include, particularly, the experience of adults who had been born of incest. We therefore repeated our invitation to social workers asking specifically about the experience of adults. From this we received information from three more social workers about four young adults, bringing our total number of cases to ten. Because of organisational changes and other commitments, analysis of the material was interrupted at this stage. A research grant four years later allowed us to do a follow-up of the cases, a full literature search and to complete the analysis.

In the following chapters, we shift our focus from considering general issues about incest to describing the experience of real people in daily living and in professional situations. The knowledge we have obtained has its limitations, but it is a starting point for further exploration of the issues which affect the lives of children born of incest. A social worker in a lifetime of work with children and families may meet very few such children. By bringing together the case examples of several social workers, however, we have begun to build a knowledge base and to describe a pattern of the dynamics and reactions between the children, their families and friends, which have relevance for the practice of social work and other child care professionals. The preconceptions and half-truths that abound in the area of incest are those that would influence decisions in the case studies we describe. It is easy to see with hindsight that other decisions might or could have had a better outcome for the child concerned. The uncertainties for practice lie in the issues already presented in the previous chapters which offer a context for this study.

Data about the people in the study

The case studies reveal the complexities of the families of origin of these children; for example, the perceived difficulties of finding accepting carers for children whose situation is the product of sexual taboos, the prejudices and strong feelings of the whole community and the strength of irrational fears projected on to the children.

Basic data about the children and adults is presented opposite in Table 1. We were able to obtain follow-up information about six of the young people, thus providing us with knowledge of them over a period of at least five years. Of the four about whom we have less knowledge, our contact with one was limited to her very vivid correspondence with a social worker outside the UK, while another responded in a one-off interview to our publicised request for contact with adults who were born of incest. We have information about the telling of their origins to the remaining two from their social workers, but it did not prove possible to obtain more up-to-date information about them.

Table 1

Children and adults studied — basic data

Name	Father's relationship to Mother	Mother's age at birth of child	Age when told of origins	By whom told	Age when separated from birth mother
Peter	brother*	18	11	social worker	10 (fostered)
Andrew & John	father*	NK but was 15 when first child by father born	16 & 17	adoptive mother	3 & 4 (various homes)
Maria & Suzanne	stepfather	14	27	former social worker	under 1 (res care)
Jenny	father*	14	16½	residential carer & social worker	under 1 (fostered)
Isabel	uncle	14	16	adoptive parents & social worker	under 1 (adopted)
Pat	father*	NK	18	grandmother	under 1
Marion	stepfather	17	28	own enquiries & counsellor	under 1 (adopted)
Jack	father*	NK	28+	own enquiries & neighbours.	under 1 (fostered)

*These relationships represent criminal offences in England & Wales. All the cases would have been offences in Scotland.

43

Their backgrounds all include experience of shame, secrets, rejection and prejudice. Their existence reminded adults of adult behaviour. A range of situations was evident with regards to the identity of the father, genetic inheritance, and of social acceptance or non-acceptance of the child.

At least five of the eight birth mothers were in their teens when they bore the children, three being fourteen, one seventeen, while the fifth was fifteen when she had her first child by her father. The other three were thought to have been under 20.

All except one of the children were separated from their birth mothers at an early age. Four moved into permanent families, two remained in residential care, two followed the all too familiar trail in and out of foster homes and residential establishments until they were adopted together in their early teens. The birth mother of the ninth left home, reportedly rejected by her family, leaving her child to be brought up by a grandmother whom she believed to be her mother. The only one who had significant contact with his birth mother during childhood was admitted to care at the age of eight with a view to permanent placement, but when this placement broke down he returned to live with his mother.

Of the six in permanent families from an early age (four adopted, two fostered) at least five remained in touch with their adoptive parents or carers as adults. While the relationship of one of them with her adoptive parents was not entirely satisfactory, she maintained it until their death. The two adopted in their teens and who are now in their twenties, are in close contact with their adoptive mother in spite of serious difficulties and two others are in close touch with their foster carers. We were unable to follow up the sixth.

All the young people came from working class families. From the information we have about them, there were relatively few overt problems in these families other than that of the irregular sexual relationships, the extent of which varied from a reportedly one-off episode between brother and sister to five children born at yearly intervals to a teenage girl by her father. Three of the four children placed at an early age grew up in middle class families, as did the two boys placed in their teens, but in only one case did this fact appear to be of significance to the young person when they met their birth families (see Chapter 7).

In the main, therefore, these were children born to very young mothers in otherwise self-sufficient working class families. They were all separated from their mothers, most of them at an early age, and most were placed in middle class families with whom they have kept in close touch.

Background summaries

Although each of the histories had much in common with at least some of the others, they have been divided into three groups for the purpose of this study:
1) Those where telling about origins was part of the social work planning for them;
2) Those for whom the decision to tell arose from their disturbed behaviour during adolescence;
3) Young adults who searched for information on their own initiative.

Using these categories we have summarised the backgrounds of the young people in the study. Fictitious names have been used throughout.

Planned telling

Peter

Peter's father is his mother's slightly older brother, with whom she had a relationship when she returned home, aged 18, after breaking up with the father of her first child. Peter is small for his age and looks several years younger than he actually is. He spent his early years with his mother and half-siblings, but with frequent admissions to hospital for treatment of an unusual physical condition. His mother felt extremely guilty about this, which partly accounts for why she did not reveal the truth about Peter's parentage until he was 11 and in the care of the local authority, with a plan for early placement in a new family. The social worker then found out that his condition was not related to his incestuous conception.

Peter's birth mother felt at the time that she could not offer him the care and attention that he needed but was co-operative in preparing him for a new family. His uncle/father had never acknowledged his parenthood either to Peter or to the rest of the family and Peter had been told that a former boyfriend of his mother, whom he knew, was his father. His mother agreed that part of Peter's preparation for the new family

45

should be to tell him the truth, but the actual telling was delayed because the social worker was concerned lest Peter would not receive adequate support after the event. She herself also received helpful advice from a consultant child psychiatrist regarding how and when to tell.

John and Andrew
These two boys are the third and fourth children born to their mother by her father. Two of her five children died as infants. Eventually someone revealed the family story and the father/grandfather was imprisoned. The boys' mother then married and was re-housed, taking the two boys with her, but leaving her eldest child, a daughter, with the physically unfit grandmother. Later this girl was herself abused as an adolescent.

It soon became clear that John and Andrew's stepfather resented the presence of the two boys and they were received into care. Apart from one visit from their grandmother, they had no further contact with their birth family until after they were told the truth about their origins in later adolescence.

The boys remained in residential care for some years and were then placed with foster carers who were told their family history. The foster carers attributed subsequent difficulties with John to his origins and he was removed from foster care. Andrew remained with the foster carers for 14 months until he was admitted to hospital with possible epilepsy, which exists in his birth family but was not confirmed in Andrew. A decision was made not to return Andrew to his foster home because he was showing acute symptoms of stress. He had stopped growing and 'froze' developmentally for ten years. He joined his brother John, once more in residential care.

Aged 15 and 14 respectively, John and Andrew were placed with a single adoptive parent, herself a social worker. On the advice of a psychiatrist (who did not see the boys) it was agreed that the adoptive mother should tell them about their origins when she considered that the time was right. Psychiatric advice would be made available to her at that time. Meanwhile the boys were told that their father was much older than their mother and that he could not marry her. The adoptive mother also attempted to find out more about incest. Both boys took time to settle into their adoptive home and worked hard at this. They were antagonistic towards their birth mother, which the adoptive mother found painful. She was aware also of holding a secret that was rightfully theirs. However, it was about three years before she felt that Andrew was ready to be told. The telling took place spontaneously in the kitchen while doing domestic chores. John was soon told when he returned home from his term at college.

Maria and Suzanne

The mother of these twins followed her mother to England from Jamaica at the age of 12 after eight years of separation from her mother. A year later she was found to be pregnant, but it was not until 17 years later, that she admitted to the girls' social worker that the twins' father was her stepfather. When the twins were born, in the late 1950s, their mother requested adoption as she was too young to care for them. Some effort was made to find a black family for them, but at that time recruitment of adoptive families was not specifically aimed at the black community. When the effort failed, they were placed in a residential nursery, then in a convent children's home and eventually, following a further failure to find a foster family when they were ten, in a small children's home with a black carer. The girls remained there until they left care at 18 although the black carer had left a year after their arrival. During most of this time the girls knew nothing at all about their history, although it was apparent to the social worker who took up their case when they were eight years old that they were very keen to know about their mother. Unfortunately their mother's file had been mislaid in 1964 during major reorganisation of the local authorities.

When the girls were 17 years old information came to light about their parent's whereabouts and the social worker was able to contact both the girls' mother and their grandmother. The mother then told the social worker that her stepfather had been the father of the girls. She herself was now married with other children and she was very anxious for the security of her family if the truth were to be revealed. She did agree, however, to meet the girls once, providing that they were not told about their origins. The social worker said that she could not agree to this request, but that she would not tell them before the meeting with their mother.

47

The girls were shocked when they heard that their mother had in fact been three years younger when they were born than they were then, but the meeting went well. Photographs were shared. The mother refused further support and there were no other meetings. Six months later the girls left care. This was a very busy time for them, finding accommodation and so on, and the social worker did not think it was the right time to talk about their background. She had arranged to keep in touch with them although she had left the department. The girls moved first into a hostel and then into a rented flat. They held down good jobs and after a few years were able to buy a flat of their own. The social worker had difficulty in deciding when to tell them as there never seemed to be an occasion when they both seemed open for the information. They were in their early twenties and having tea with the social worker in her home when she felt they were both ready.

Adolescent queries
Jenny
Jenny's family lived deep in the country on a large estate, but after her birth they moved to a council house. Her father was her mother's father, and he was subsequently convicted of incest and imprisoned. Jenny was placed as a baby with foster carers who were not told the truth about her family circumstances. They were simply told that her mother was very young and that there could never be any contact between Jenny and the birth family. They were to some extent mystified as to why Jenny had not been considered suitable for adoption, and also as to why they themselves had been approved as foster carers rather than adopters. They thought this must be because they did not attend church. The foster mother was in poor health and was quite seriously disabled by the time Jenny and her elder foster brother were teenagers. There was also a natural daughter in the family, two years younger than Jenny.

By the time Jenny was 14 years old her behaviour was disruptive at home and at school. She was stealing, lying and not caring properly for herself. Eventually, she was moved into a children's home for a 'cooling off' period. At that time she talked to her new social worker and to the residential worker about her strong wish to know about her mother. She had been told what the foster carers knew, and what they had deduced

- that the family lived in the country and were poor. The social worker, who was aware of the truth about Jenny's origins from the information on the file, decided that she must be told the truth but that this should be done over time together with some more comprehensive sex education than she had so far received and some life story work. The next few months were spent on this work, including visits to significant places. The social worker also met Jenny's mother and grandmother who were anxious to co-operate. By that time her mother was now married with three sons.

Isabel

Isabel's family came to England from Jamaica. Her conception was the result of a liaison between her teenage mother and a middle-aged uncle. He was subsequently prosecuted and imprisoned. The family blamed the mother for the disgrace that was caused by the crime committed and the involvement of the law. They made it clear that she could not return home with her baby, so Isabel was placed in a residential nursery. The birth mother stayed in contact for about two and a half years, but there seems to have been no serious effort to help her to plan for the baby's future. Two years later the mother became pregnant again by a boyfriend. This baby was also placed in the same nursery, and six months later the mother stopped visiting and indicated that she thought she would never be able to provide for her children.

Shortly after Isabel was five it was decided that she would be placed separately from her sister and she moved to her adoptive family which was white. The sisters have remained in touch, but do not have a close relationship.

Isabel's white adoptive parents were well educated and highly committed to help Isabel understand and appreciate her cultural and family background. They were told the facts about her birth, but given no encouragement to tell Isabel at an appropriate time. In fact, they appear to have received very little support from the agency at the time of the placement.

In her mid-teens, Isabel appeared to be an unhappy and disaffected young person. Her adoptive family approached the social worker they knew to be in touch with her sister asking her whether she could help

Isabel make some sense of her past. The social worker felt at first that the adoptive parents should do the telling in order to demonstrate their sense of responsibility and therefore promote trust, but in retrospect she reported feeling that she was expecting too much of them in the stressful situation in which the family found itself at the time. We have been unable to update information about Isabel.

Adult searchers

Pat

Pat discovered at the age of 18 that her father was her mother's father. She had been brought up by her grandmother, believing that she was her mother, and when at the age of 18 she wanted to get married and obtained a copy of her birth certificate, she discovered that this was not so. Upon being challenged, her grandmother told her the truth. According to Pat, the birth family rejected her mother shortly after her birth with the result that the mother left home.

Pat contacted a social worker a few years after she had discovered the facts of her birth, because she had experienced a broken relationship and felt that she was having acute difficulties in achieving personal relationships. The social worker was able to counsel her in her dealings with her mother and grandmother, but we have been unable to obtain updated information on Pat's progress.

Marion

The information that we have about Marion is based on correspondence between her and a post-adoption counsellor in an English speaking country outside the UK. She gave permission for us to use this correspondence as she was interested in the working party's project.

Marion discovered when attempting to trace her birth family that her father had been her mother's stepfather. She was adopted as a young baby into a middle-class family and it seems that her adoptive parents had minimal information about her origins. She does not describe her adoptive placement as unsatisfactory, but neither does she seem to have had a very close relationship with her adoptive parents, especially her father. She gives the impression that her adoptive mother lacked confidence in her role when confronted with a growing daughter asking questions about her birth family. This may be why Marion, who writes that she had always been curious about her origins, waited until after the death of both her adoptive parents before she began to trace her birth parents. Her birth parents had three children, one of whom, a boy, was placed with her in the same adoptive family. She describes him briefly in the correspondence, saying that she never got on well with him and that he was extremely difficult as a young boy, later being assessed as having 'psychotic tendencies'. Her full sister was placed for adoption in another family, and she succeeded in tracing her first. This she describes as an extremely fulfilling experience, although, she says, she and her sister are two very different people.

Jack

Jack responded to the BAAF working party's appeal for information from adults born as a result of incest. He had been unable to discover for certain the identity of his father, who could have been either his mother's father or her brother. He was placed as a young baby with long-term foster carers whom he looks upon as his parents. He did not talk about his feelings as a boy, but said that he was impelled to search for his origins when he himself became a father. He discovered that his mother had been admitted to a hospital for the mentally disabled at his birth and that this was why he had grown up with a foster family. He had been unable to obtain precise information about her admission. A social worker who visited her told him that she had denied all knowledge of him and refused any discussion.

Jack decided to take matters into his own hands. He discovered his mother's original address, went to this address and called at the house next door. He told the people there why he was making enquiries.

Concluding comments on the histories

In presenting the case material we have been influenced in several ways. The material was not part of a planned research study aimed at understanding all the implications for all parties to this situation. It is retrospective and relies on the case records, diaries and memories of carers and social workers. The information is therefore uneven and the material quoted has been edited both consciously and unconsciously by its authors. There is, however, a basic integrity about it which it is hoped comes through in the following chapters.

Readers can hypothesise as to how they would have done the 'telling' or made the decision not to tell; what other developmental issues and interlocking factors need to be considered; what support they would have offered to the children and sought for themselves. Their views about this will be influenced by their own professional discipline, orientation and experience. Here we present a social work perspective. We do not know the orientation of each particular social worker, but we do know they each had much practice experience in statutory social work agencies in the UK, and were ready to give time and effort in sharing this with us during the project.

Reference

1 DoH circular LAC(84)3 Guidance to Adoption Agency Regulations 83 para 86.

5 The case studies: planned telling

In this chapter, we give extracts from the case histories of children and young people for whom the telling was planned. In each case details are given of who did the telling, why and how it was done at a particular time and the reported reactions of the children, their carers and the social worker involved.

Peter

For Peter, aged 11 and still in contact with his birth mother, telling was part of the work in preparing for a new family. His birth mother 'agreed with me (social worker) that he should be told and expressed a strong wish to be involved in telling him.' In the event she did not keep the appointment made and the social worker talked to Peter on her own.

With regard to Peter's previous knowledge his social worker writes:

'His mother always maintained that his father was a man with whom she had a brief relationship. This man never lived with her after Peter's birth, never provided her with any support and therefore had no relationship with Peter. However, he had seen Peter two or three times...and Peter had been told that this man was his father. Peter never talked about his father with me and showed no interest in the subject when I broached it.'

Peter had spent his early years with his mother and had been in contact with her throughout his time in care. He did not raise the subject of his origins with her, but one day when his uncle/father visited unexpectedly, he said in his mother's but no-one else's presence 'Hello, you're my dad aren't you?' The man neither replied to nor denied the statement. It seems he has maintained this attitude over the past six years, although Peter's aternity is now acknowledged within the family.

Peter's social worker planned the telling session carefully.

'I decided to hold the session with Peter in our children's workroom in my office. I felt this would give us the best opportunity to be uninterrupted and also allow me to use whatever materials and props I needed to help during the session. I had in advance prepared a family tree of all his mother's family and their offspring. I had also prepared a small diagram of his mother's relationships and the children resulting from those relationships.

'Peter knew that our session that day was concerned with his birth family. His foster mother informed me that four days previously Peter had had a long and painful outburst of pent-up feelings of anger and rejection. He had also expressed confusion about who was who in his family. Whilst not mentioning his own father he had said that he didn't know who his brother's father was.

'Peter had anticipated and thought about our meeting. When he arrived he didn't want to talk with me about his outburst but I acknowledged and accepted the feelings and views that he had expressed. It enabled me to move straight into the session and I knew that I had his attention. I explained that we would be stopping after a while to have a drink and a biscuit and at the end of our session we would be going to have lunch together. I started by showing Peter the chart I had made of his extended family. He was extremely interested in this...I moved on to talk generally about people getting married, or having partners, and having children. I pointed out that all his aunties and uncles and his mum had found someone they wanted to love and have babies with...I asked him whether he thought he would like to do this one day and he said he would. I asked him whether this was likely to be someone who was already in his family or outside it. He was definite about the latter and I said that that was what usually happened. We talked about how and where he might meet someone when he was grown up, where he might want to live, etc. He said he did not know how babies were born and I went on to describe this to him as simply as possible....I drew a clear distinction between this kind of love and the love we give to our mum or a sister or brother, auntie or uncle.

'Peter was very attentive during this part of the session and asked questions though he concentrated on doodling on a piece of paper, avoiding looking too directly at my illustration. I then got the chart that I had made of his mother's relationships and children. I told how she had met her first boyfriend and how she had loved him and they had made a baby together, his brother. I went on to say that things had not worked out and she had come back to her home to her mother. I told him how unhappy and lonely she had been when she returned home. Living at home too was her brother, Peter's uncle, and he was also feeling lonely and unhappy. Because they were both unhappy and lonely they started loving each other and making each other happier in a way they should not have done. They made a baby together and that baby was Peter.

'Everybody's first dad is the man who puts his seed inside their mother and that means that Peter's uncle was his first dad. I said that his mum had wanted to tell him this for a long time but didn't do so because she was frightened because she knew that it was something that she and his uncle shouldn't have done...but this didn't stop her loving Peter and it was not something that he should feel bad about. It did not make him a bad or a naughty boy. I went on to say "because this happened to you doesn't mean that people won't love you if they know about it. The people who know, like your foster mother and me, haven't changed our view of you as a smashing boy. But it's probably something you might like to keep quite private, just to tell to people you know well and whom you like a lot. Something special about you that you just want them to know or people who are going to be very important to you like your new family".'

During Peter's session with his social worker, the latter described his reactions thus.

'He had been rapt in attention and I asked him if he understood and had any questions. He seemed unsure and demonstrated by one question that he had not been able to take in fully what I had said. At the same time he looked relieved and relaxed. I decided this was the moment to finish this session, it had lasted two hours and I realised that Peter, normally a fidgety child with a short

concentration span, had sat in one chair throughout. He had avoided a lot of direct eye contact but he had listened and I think had "heard" what I was saying. I asked him to tell me any time that he wanted to talk about it again and that I knew that his foster mother would also talk about it with him any time he wished. He might also like to talk to his mum when he saw her next.

'We finished the session by glueing, at his request, the two charts I had made of his family into his life story book. I said I was pleased at how well he had listened to something really important that I had wanted to tell him for some time. We went off and had lunch together at MacDonalds. He seemed more relaxed with me than he had been for some months. We returned together to his foster mother who I told in front of him what we'd been talking about. Peter went off happily to play.'

Peter moved into a new family shortly after the telling, but after four months it ended abruptly following an incident between Peter and his new sister.

'Apart from the usual questions and concerns about such an incident, I was of course deeply worried about whether my work with Peter had led him to believe consciously or unconsciously that it was alright for brothers and sisters to have sex together. I will probably never know the answer to this question. Following the disruption of his placement, Peter was rehabilitated with his birth family. One concern about this plan was whether he would interpret this move as meaning that such behaviour was acceptable within his own family (he has three younger sisters). Work was done with Peter and his mother on this and there is no evidence at all that he had behaved inappropriately with anyone within the family or outside it.'

The feelings of Peter's carers

Peter's short-term foster carer at the time of the telling was aware of the circumstances of his birth and at first felt that 'perhaps he should never be told – doesn't he have enough to cope with?' Later she was ready to co-operate with the social worker in following up the telling, but in the event Peter did not raise the issue with her. Subsequently Peter's prospective adopters were also told and seemed to accept the implications, but when Peter and their adoptive daughter were found apparently attempting sexual intercourse, the foster father asked for his immediate removal.

The feelings of Peter's social worker
Peter's social worker wrote after the telling interview:

> *'In the end, telling him turned out to be easier than I had expected; like any secret, once it was spoken it just became much less awful. That is not to say I don't recognise it may be just that the burden has now been taken off my shoulders and put onto Peter who, after all, has to live with this for the rest of his life. However, it is still very clear to me that it was right that Peter should be told now, however little at this point he may take in and understand. Because now it is not a secret, it is not something that is going to be blurted out at him in some dreadful way in a moment of stress, for instance, by his mother or another member of the family or by his new family.'*

John and Andrew

John and Andrew, third and fourth children of their mother by her father, had remained with the birth mother until they were four and three and then had several placements until they were placed for adoption at the ages of 15 and 14 respectively. Their single adoptive mother had agreed as part of the initial planning for the placement, 'that when the right time occurred I would be prepared to tell them who their father was and what was known about their origins. Meanwhile a cover story was worked out and they were told that their father was an older, married man and that there could never have been any question of their mother and father being able to marry each other.'

Andrew, the younger boy, became increasingly preoccupied with why he was with adoptive parents. His adoptive mother writes:

> *'This began to loom very large with him and I could see that it really was that last piece that he felt he needed to put into the jigsaw of his life, and that not having the vital remaining information was*

holding him back. I knew the time was approaching when he needed to be told and I had a sort of preparatory talk with him about difficult things and whether he found it easy to talk to me about them, etc. Then one time we were in the kitchen, he was sitting at the table and I was busy at the sink and he repeated his desire to know who had made the decision about his first coming into care. I felt that the right moment had come, so I took a deep breath and said a quick prayer and got stuck into it.'

The adoptive mother told Andrew's older brother, John, by now at training college, when he next came home. She writes that she began telling Andrew by saying:

'...that we knew that his father had been an older married man and that I did know who he was: it was his grandfather. What had happened was that his wife had had eight children and had become ill and indeed several years later died from a long-standing heart complaint. He was very much a family man and didn't want to look outside the family for someone to love and so he had loved their mother and together they had had the five babies. The family were all very close and united and everyone kept the secret. As the mother had all her babies at home it was very hard for outsiders to find out what was happening. Within the family things must have been difficult at times to know who was in charge, who was the parent and who was responsible for the care of the children. Was it the mother who was so young or was it the grandmother?

'It must have been difficult for his grandmother if she was not well and for his mother because she was so young...Someone eventually went to the police and told them who the father of all the children was, and the family secret came out into the open. The father was taken to court and indeed went to prison. The fact that the secret was out was a great release to his mother, whose life up to then must have been very difficult; she must have loved her dad yet known that it was not right for him to be making all these babies with her. Maybe she was angry with him as well as loving him, and angry with her mother for not protecting her more. Anyway, at last she had the chance to make her own life and have

*friends outside the family and she met her husband and they fell
in love and he wanted to marry her. So they got married and she
wanted to make a home for the two boys and tried her best, but it
was very hard for her husband as seeing them kept reminding him
of the family secret and he just didn't feel happy or comfortable
about it, so that was why he asked if the boys could come into care.'*

Reaction to the telling

Andrew, sitting in the kitchen with his adoptive mother, reacted in the
following way.

*'He took all this in very quietly, listening intently, and did not ask
many questions except how long did his grandfather/father go to
prison for? He seemed to want me to go on talking about it. Some
of the time I sat with him and some of the time I carried on with
various things as I went over it all again for him...I tried to get him
to talk about how he felt about this information but he did not seem
to want to. I tried to get round this by asking him how he thought
John would take it and whether he would understand it in the way
that he, Andrew, did but nothing much would draw him. He
remained very calm and continued sitting very comfortably at the
table and I hugged him and told him some nice things about
himself, and how this was the last piece of the jigsaw of his past,
but now he was making his own life...He did seem visibly relaxed
and relieved that this was all there was to know.'*

His brother John's main reaction on being given the information was to
ask whether this meant that he could now get to see his older sister. At a
later date Andrew developed a physical problem that might have required
treatment and he became interested, rather than anxious, about whether
the circumstances of his birth would have any relevance. In the end the
problem turned out to be minor and his parentage was not relevant.

After John and Andrew learnt about their origins:

*'They started to talk a lot more about their mother and how they
felt about her, which was still very angry. When I tried to discuss
this in the light of the new information...Andrew, in particular,*

insisted that it was all her fault and that even at fourteen she should have said no. Any attempts to discuss how impossible this must have been, how mixed her feelings about her father must have been, met with a stone wall.'

A little while later they met their mother. This was an impromptu visit, when the adoptive mother felt that it was needed, and was somewhat difficult at first, but the boys and their mother relaxed as time passed.

'As the ice was broken, and I felt that this was the only chance I might ever have of getting confirmation from her of the truth of what I had told the boys, I decided to dive straight in. So I said that the boys did now know all about themselves and that their father was also her father; this was true wasn't it? She agreed, and did not seem upset that I said this, so I told her that in explaining things to the boys I had told them that she was very young when everything had started, and that it must have been a very difficult time for her.

'She seemed very relieved and told me that she had had a terrible childhood, that she did not have any happy memories of it, that all her life she had been a drudge and felt put upon and that she had felt like a prisoner...I said that it must have been a great relief to her when her father went to prison and she had the chance to build her own life. She agreed. I said that she must have been very sad that things didn't work out when she and her husband tried to make a home for the boys. She became rather defensive about this. She was very willing for me to take a photo of her for the boys and posed with John beside her in the back of the car. It became a rather pleasant social occasion and she left giving us her telephone number, telling the boys to keep in touch and John to get a job...

'The boys seemed very relieved that we had met her, pleased to talk about how nice she was, to go over the confirmation that she had given us of the past, to agree with me that it was very sad what she had told us about how she felt about her childhood. I think that John found it quite exciting, particularly as we were going to be able to have his sister's address, and he frequently asked me if I had heard anything. Andrew found it harder to change his

perception of her, and only grudgingly shifted slightly...The boys took pride in the photo and in my telling people that she looked like Andrew but had John's extrovert personality.'

Later the boys met their sister and John met their father. The adoptive parent described their response.

'Both boys continued to blame their mother and would not accept that she was very young and needed to be protected by their father, not abused by him. Any contact with their birth family always seemed to reinforce this opinion as the other part of the family had ostracised her. John said that their father, too, thought that their mother was at fault in some way.'

The feelings of the boys' carers were discussed by the adoptive mother.

'There was much debate about whether the first foster carers should be told about the incest and in the end they were; the foster mother found this information hard to bear, and when there were difficulties with John she attributed them to his parentage and she rejected him. Andrew remained in the foster home for a further fourteen months and then the stress he was under became too much for him and he was admitted to hospital...It was decided at a case conference in the hospital that he should not return to the foster home, but join John in the children's home. This decision was a severe trauma to Andrew and he stopped growing and learning and remained developmentally "frozen".'

Concerning her own feelings, earlier in the placement, the adoptive mother writes:

'I did find it hard that I knew something important that they did not know, but equally, given the fact that they did not know it, I didn't feel at gut level that the right time had yet come to tell them.'

Continuing about her feelings after she had told them:

'The marvellous thing is that it is now out in the open, that we are all feeling pretty comfortable with it, it's no big deal...For my part the best thing is that I no longer know something that they don't

know; it's as if we are walking about in the sunshine and fresh air, instead of boxed in a room with a cupboard that is about to disgorge some terrible taboo secret!'

Later, she thought about who else should be told:

'It has always been clear to me that there would be certain people who just never would feel comfortable with the information. I have tended to regard the information as very confidential, but that there might be people who could handle it and support one through its difficulties. Just how difficult it is to assess who these might be came home to me very early on, even before the boys came to me, when a friend whom I told and who I thought had liberal attitudes said it was very bad blood that would come out...Perhaps because I am a social worker and as people say "used to all that sort of thing" I might have underestimated just how much to the rest of the world it is a definite taboo subject, and many many people will never have come across it or will have invested energy in repressing or denying knowledge. I can say that when things got really difficult with John, I was very glad that it was not widely known amongst all the friends and relations who I called upon to help me, and whose continued care for John was important.'

Maria and Suzanne

Maria and Suzanne's social worker first knew them when they were eight years old and remained in contact with them long after she left the agency and they had left care. The social worker writes:

'Maria and Suzanne grew up knowing virtually nothing about their history. When I became their social worker in 1967 their first question to me was "Do you know where our mummy is?" There was nothing on their file except the mother's name and age. The mother's case file had been lost during a reorganisation. Attempts at that time to find out more were unsuccessful. We could not even tell the girls precisely where they came from, although we thought it likely that their parents had emigrated from the Caribbean, as subsequently turned out to be the case.'

The social worker was unable to trace their family until they were seventeen and then discovered that their mother had been abused by her stepfather. Because of secrecy within the family around this, even after more than seventeen years, the social worker respected the mother's strong wishes and did not explain the whole truth to the girls at that stage. Her focus at that time was on promoting a meeting between the girls and their mother, which would not have been possible had she not promised to withhold the full truth until they were eighteen years old. After leaving care the sisters remained very close, almost to the point of exclusiveness, and they held down good jobs, seeming content in their lifestyle.

Maria and Suzanne were given the information in the context of one of many informal visits to the social worker's home after they had left care and she had left the agency. As she considered them to be intelligent young adults, she gave them the facts directly and without embellishment. The social worker writes:

'It was several years before the subject came up in a way that made me feel that the right moment had come. Several times previously I had talked about their mother but each time one or the other of them showed that they did not want to talk. This time both of them were attentive and so I just told them that there was information about their father which they had a right to know.'

The girls' first reactions to information about their origins was severe criticism of their father and keen sympathy for their mother. Several years later, the social worker was able to show them their mother's file, which:

'...contained answers from their mother to questions about a whole variety of things. When asked "who do you like" she replied "I like my father because he is kind to me". To the question "who do you not like" she replied "my mother because she is strict." Now at last Maria and Suzanne have accepted their past as best they can. They realise that one parent can't be all good and the other all bad.'

The social worker's feelings about the telling
Maria and Suzanne's social worker thinks that their case would have been handled differently had they been children today.

'The dates as well as the time scales are significant here. I do not think that this story could happen now. Firstly, an adoptive family could not be found for the girls in 1959 and so they grew up in residential care. That made a difference to my thinking about the case. Secondly, although recording is often woefully inadequate now, I hope that there would not be such total blanks about children's histories. The third point is that I treated it as we then treated cases of incest...By the time I finally told the girls in the early 1980s, I was able to put it in the context of child abuse rather than incest. That made a difference to my thinking about the case – whether it made any difference to the girls I am not sure. The facts were the same either way.

'With hindsight I feel that I should have told the girls the whole story in 1976, whatever their mother said. Shielding them from part of the story was wrong. They would have needed help in handling so much at once but they could have coped...I do not believe, however, that it would have become possible for Maria and Suzanne to establish a continuing relationship with their mother – the family secrets ran too deep. Again I was dragged into this. I kept the secret of their paternity for several years and was not easy in my mind about this. I do not believe that they would have approached the agency for information and I therefore felt myself to be the sole possessor of a secret that was really theirs.'

6 The case studies: adolescent queries

Two adolescent girls feature in this chapter. Their carers were concerned about their disturbed and evident unhappiness. Details are presented of the social workers' assessment of each situation, the action that they took and the reactions of the adolescent and her carers. The social workers offer their own reflective comments on the outcome.

Jenny

Jenny was in residential care following breakdown of the foster placement she had been in since birth, and talked to her social worker, who writes regarding:

> '...her confusion about her very strong wish to know about her mother. She seemed to have both idealised fantasies and negative ones, for instance, she thought her mother would be fat and ugly (this is how she saw herself). I told her I would do what I could to help her.'

Jenny had been told that her birth mother was young and poor. Her curiosity about her was overwhelming as she grew older. Her social worker spent a few months building up a relationship with her and doing some life story work. She wrote as follows when Jenny was about sixteen and a half.

> 'I spent a day in the children's home where I and the residential worker could concentrate entirely on Jenny. The residential worker had been talking to her about sexual relationships and found her knowledge very patchy. I told Jenny I had seen her mother and that her mother and her grandmother were very keen to meet her but that we all agreed that she should know all about her family background before this should happen. I gave her a photograph

of her relatives who looked what they are – charming respectable people. I told her I wanted to tell her about her father. I referred to her knowledge of sexual intercourse using those words and how we had been talking to her about a sexual relationship between men and women who love each other. I said she would know that that kind of love was different from the kind of love between parents and children. She talked a little about this (her relationship with her foster father was quite good). I then told her that it sometimes happened that between members of a family the love became sexual and that sexual intercourse could happen. I asked her if she had ever heard of this. She said "no" in an amazed way and seemed to have no emotional response to the concept. I then told her that this happens more often than people realise and this is what had happened in her case, so that her mother's father was in fact her father too. The residential worker and I went on to talk about these kinds of relationships but we did not use the word incest.'

Towards the end of the interview with Jenny the social worker said that other people might find the story quite a shock.

'She did not seem to be upset...She could not wait to show her photograph to other members of staff. She told them all the whole story without embarrassment or inhibition. Later in the day we advised that some people might not find the story acceptable and that she should be careful before telling outsiders. We went into town and had some tea, and then came back to the children's home. Most of her conversation was about her planned meeting with her mother but she reverted back to the subject of her father and grandfather...Sometime later Jenny asked more questions about daughters and fathers. She talked about her foster father and I was able to say that this is how fathers and daughters ought to be but sadly things went wrong sometimes.

'Six months after the telling interview Jenny heard girls at work talking about incest. They said that children born as a result were always "mental". She reported that she just moved away from them, but as soon as she returned to the children's home she told me and one of the workers what had happened. We talked about old wives'

tales but also that there were reasons why incest was forbidden in the first place. This is the first time I find the word incest recorded in my notes of conversations with Jenny. I also recorded that she was slowly coming to realise the implications.'

Meanwhile Jenny's behaviour had once more deteriorated. A short spell in the original foster home ended disastrously, but in spite of this contact was maintained throughout.

Jenny's main preoccupation in adolescence was with her birth mother. She did in fact establish a relationship with her and with her grandmother, visiting them regularly during the year after the telling session. Her social worker writes:

'Jenny told me that during a weekend staying with her mother, she had seen her father over the fence in his garden but he would not look up. I explained that he must feel guilty and ashamed and that I had heard from her grandmother that he never talked about his feelings to anyone and she had never been able to discuss what had happened with him. A little later when she was staying with the family and went to the grandmother's house he came in. The mother introduced Jenny to him but he walked straight past her and out of the back door. There is much in my records at this time of conversations with the mother and grandmother who told me a great deal of what they had been through, and in the mother's case what had haunted her ever since. Eight months after the telling, Jenny was feeling torn between her interests in her new family and guilt about her foster parents. By then she was not visiting either family and visits to her birth family petered out.'

The feelings of Jenny's carers

Jenny's foster carers, with whom she had been placed as a baby, knew her mother's name and age and were told simply that there could never be any contact between her and her family. They were not told of the circumstances of Jenny's birth.

When the social worker had talked to Jenny at the children's home about her origins, she wrote:

'I discussed with Jenny the need for her foster parents to know the facts and she asked me to tell them as soon as possible, but not to tell her foster brother and sister. The next day I called and saw the foster parents together. They had some idea that I wanted to talk about Jenny's background and about meeting her first mother but had no idea at all about the incest. They had seen a programme on the television about the subject and had been talking about it, otherwise they seemed to have no knowledge or experience about it.

'The foster father remembered that the agency had been unwilling for him to look after the children when his wife went into hospital. He had apparently been told that if the children were older it would not be permitted for a man to look after a foster daughter. Our discussion re-evoked his angry feelings about that. The foster mother was hurt and angry that all the social workers who had visited her during sixteen years had known but had not explained. She said there had always been a mystery about why Jenny needed to be looked after, and she also said it would have been more natural for her to have told Jenny rather than social workers. The relationship between Jenny and her foster carers was strained at this time. I suggested that the foster mother should ring Jenny in the evening to reassure her that they were not affected by the information and they did this and had a tearful conversation, agreeing that the two other children should be told the story. I had recorded that, in an earlier conversation, the foster mother had talked about a mystery in Jenny's background and had some ideas which were not far from the truth.'

Jenny's social worker, after the telling session with the residential social worker, writes:

'We thought afterwards that our attempts both to describe what had happened in terms of a love that went wrong but also to say that the act itself between father and daughter was wrong was more to do with our need than with Jenny's.'

Isabel
Isabel's adoptive parents, with whom she had lived since she was five,

approached a social worker already known to them, because, at sixteen years, she was 'obviously an unhappy, disaffected non-achieving young person.' She had been told that her mother was a very young, unsupported girl who had had an unplanned baby. The adoptive parents, however, were aware of the full facts when she was first placed with them but were given no counselling or support regarding whether and when to tell Isabel. The social worker writes:

'They were highly committed to help her understand and appreciate her racial origins, as well as her cultural and family background. However, they reached a sticking point about telling her about the circumstances of her conception. They felt troubled about the dual issue of incest and crime...They had nowhere to go for advice. I think that they would have been open to telling at an early stage if they had had the support and confirmation that this was best.'

The social worker continues, regarding Isabel's sessions with her:

'She came to see me reluctantly...she barely communicated for several sessions. Nevertheless, I assumed that the fact that she put in an appearance at all indicated a strong impulse to find out more about herself. She gave the impression of being a frozen child, with a very poor self image. My understanding of the situation was that first she was still stuck at more or less the five-year-old stage. The traumatic events of that time had never been adequately resolved. Second, although she was in many ways coversant with the facts about her past she was muddled about the details, feeling negative about the story...and suspicious that some information was being held back. I decided that dealing with the first was necessary before any progress could be made on the second. This involved encouraging her to do work with me aimed at helping her to develop her sense of awareness of herself, and helping her parents to understand where and why she was stuck...

'It soon became clear that she could not reconcile herself to the lack of information about her birth father, mainly because she sensed a worrying secret.'

This social worker encouraged Isabel's parents to explain the facts to her.

'I hoped that it would re-establish trust between them. We discussed the mechanics of telling, and I advised them to acknowledge that they had postponed it as they found the facts upsetting themselves and had wanted to protect her...It would have been preferable to wait for a more natural cue, for instance, a TV programme or a newspaper article, but there was no way of predicting when this would present itself.'

Subsequently Isabel's social worker wrote:

'In retrospect, I think perhaps I could have remained in control of the telling by bringing it into my life story work, perhaps with parents present. I think, in their anxiety, they rushed it.'

She added that, when Isabel came to see her after her parents had informed her, she wanted confirmation of the information.

'I did this by recreating her birth parents' story as best I could. I tried to convey that the circumstances in which they found themselves were understandable, although their solution to the difficulties had been wrong. We discussed legal definitions of incest and the way they vary from society to society. My focus was helping her to "own" her own story.

'Isabel's reactions (to the birth information) were mixed; she was relieved to have a mystery cleared, she transferred her negative feelings from her birth mother to her birth father, and she needed repeated reassurance about the implications for herself, that is, whether she would go mad being the child of relatives.'

7 The case studies: adult searchers

This chapter tells the stories of the three adults in this study, and how they discovered the facts about their origins through their own enquiries, two of them without social work support.

Pat

Of these three Pat discovered about her origins inadvertently. She obtained her full birth certificate when she planned to marry and eventually her grandmother, who had brought her up and whom she believed to be her mother, told her the truth. We have no details regarding how she was told, nor do we know what her initial reaction was to the information her grandmother gave her. We do know that she realised that she had been treated differently from the rest of the family as she grew up, and that she also experienced a sense of rejection which, upon hearing the truth, she associated with the rejection of her mother. When she discovered the truth she felt bitter towards her grandmother but very protective towards her mother who she discovered was living in another town. She then set about an attempt to reconcile her mother and her grandmother, later describing this as "almost like a crusade". She achieved some success in this, although her mother never moved back to the home town. In the course of these efforts Pat seems to some extent to have been able to reconcile herself to her own origins.

Marion

Marion has written vividly to her counsellor about her feelings concerning her origins. Adopted as a baby along with her brother but separated from her sister, she became intensely interested in her birth parents during her adolescence.

> 'Now I was interested in what sort of people they were. What made them tick? Did they ever think about me? What were their

occupations? What happened that they felt I should be placed in another home?

'My adoptive mother explained that my parents weren't able to cope with three children and my mother felt it in her children's interest to find them a family that could offer them more...She (the adoptive mother) always said I was kind of special.'

As she grew older, Marion came to think of the term 'special' negatively.

Marion describes her brother as having been 'very difficult' as they grew up, and he eventually left home without leaving an address before the death of the adoptive parents when Marion and he were in their late twenties. It was after their death that Marion felt that the time was right to begin her search for her birth family and she contacted a social worker who supported her in tracing first her sister and then her mother.

Marion discovered through her social worker counsellor that:

'My mother was raped by my father who was married to my grandmother (he was her stepfather). She was seventeen when I was born and educationally very limited. She has subsequently moved to (another town) and married and has two sons.'

The discovery of these facts did not inhibit Marion from continuing with her search and she writes:

'I was very excited and hyped up, also quite anxious and apprehensive, confused. So many mixed emotions at once.'

Marion had traced and met her sister before hearing from her mother.

'It is such an incredible experience when you meet a blood sibling that you can't even remember. It's enriched my whole life. Probably altered my life a bit too.'

After a long and frustrating wait, Marion at last heard from her birth mother.

'It's funny but after reading her letter I first experienced a feeling of resentment (quite weird!) and then a deep sort of sadness which still seems to persist. At the moment I am feeling quite depressed, which is unusual for me – but I put these feelings down to a

confusion of many feelings and perhaps not quite knowing how to
cope with this whole situation.

'In my reply letter to her, I told her a lot about myself and
stressed the fact that I don't hold her responsible at all for what
happened. I feel this is important so as not to make her feel guilty
(which I suspect she does feel). We're obviously on two very
different social levels and this actually worries me quite a bit. Will
this interfere with things when we do meet? I know it's rather a
minor, silly thing to worry about, but there you have it.'

Later she and her sister met her mother.

'I think the emotions I underwent were at first a strange wonder
that this stranger was indeed my mother. Then I felt the beginning
of acceptance, then after the visit to Granny I felt bewildered and
then angry that somewhere along the line someone was lying. Then
I just felt indifferent towards everybody and I still do. A strange
sort of distancing of myself from them. I'm sure it will pass though.'

When Marion and her sister visited their mother, the "different social
levels" became more evident. This may have been why the sisters only
remained with their mother and her family for a short while and then,
on impulse, decided to visit their grandmother. Here they found a very
different version from their mother's, which was that she had been forced
repeatedly to have sexual intercourse with her stepfather. The grandmother's version was that their mother was in love with her stepfather
and in addition had willingly given up her three children for adoption as
she "couldn't be bothered to look after them". This left Marion with two
conflicting stories made the more distressing by the fact that the mother
and grandmother refused to meet and attempt to resolve the disagreement.

Marion does not know whether her adoptive parents, who died before
she started her search, were aware that her father was her step-grandfather.
It is likely that they knew very little. Certainly the past had worried her
adoptive mother:

'She would sometimes get tearful and often told me not to harp too
much on the past. She never really just let me say exactly what I
felt about my own parents. They were past history not to be dug up.'

Marion still persists in trying to trace her brother, in spite of her earlier antagonism towards him.

Jack

Jack, who was in foster care from babyhood, felt compelled to find out more about his family history when he married and had his own children; neither he nor his foster parents had any substantial information about his birth family. After a long trail, he found his birth mother's former address. When he called on the people living next door he was received kindly. He told his counsellor:

> 'They said "We believe you are who you say you are". She (the neighbour) kept looking at me. My instincts told me that she knew something. He (the neighbour's husband) said "Have you been told anything? It wasn't very pleasant Jack – it was believed that your mother had a relationship with her brother...He was convicted in the court and sent to an approved school. You do not look anything like the person supposed to be your father. It was always believed by neighbours that the real father was your grandad. You look like him. The brother was very backward and was used as the fallguy".'

Jack, who was not professionally supported during his search and who describes his GP as unsympathetic, was deeply shocked by the information he received from the neighbours.

> 'I was prepared for everything except incest. My wife was sitting out in the car while I went in – I did not know how to tell her. She and I were worried about the consequences for our children...I thought I was prepared for anything...I had a few tears that night and the following night I felt tarnished, unclean. How could I tell my mother and stepfather (foster parents)?'

His concern seemed to be around the uncertainty of the information as much as around the incest itself, especially when an uncle, whose address the neighbours had provided, refused to talk to him. As he expressed it:

> 'It's not curiosity, but a wish to know, it cannot be right for a child to go through life wishing to know. I could have coped if I'd been

told anything near the truth...I have not known who was my next of kin. Nothing to relate to in my past. My wife is sympathetic but she gets tired of it.'

Jack felt very keenly about the ignorance of the family with whom he had lived since babyhood, perhaps as keenly as he did about his own ignorance.

'What should have happened was that the agency should have told my foster mother – it would have been fairer at the outset. My foster mother should have decided when to tell me. Whatever you do there is a risk but you must be honest because it affects people in later life...It was when I had children I wanted to know about my background...I am disappointed in the way the social people handled it. Mum ought to have been able to decide what and when (I still speak to her every day) to tell me. Dad and her are surprised that I've left it (his search) *so long.'*

Jack remained distressed. He had received his information suddenly, from strangers and with no professional support.

'I feel in a worse dilemma now. There are two sets of circumstamces – an uncle who doesn't want to know me and a mother who has disowned me, but they both have different versions. I feel frustrated that it has always got to me. I never accepted that this was the end of the story. My heart says nobody rejects babies for a good reason. I wouldn't myself.'

Jack's search experience has reactivated feelings of distress as he grew up; he describes these as "always a sense of not quite belonging", for instance, the comings and goings of various social workers, the fact that the council's cheques stopped coming when he was 18. He remarked that he will have to make a will because his foster mother could not claim on his estate. The impression given is that Jack had been offered little consistent support during a most difficult and significant period of his life.

8 What emerged at follow-up

Four years after our initial discussions with their social workers we were able to obtain follow-up information on four of the young people involved. Those who had told them about their origins wrote to us as follows.

Peter: (planned telling)
Peter was placed for adoption after the telling and later, after the adoption placement broke down, he had returned to his birth mother. Peter, at sixteen, had made reasonbly steady progress within his birth family. He readily agreed to a visit from his former social worker, who wrote:

> *'He adopted an "I'm alright Jack" chirpy front, full of snappy wise cracks which made him seem about nine and ninety years all at the same time...I asked him how he felt about his father's attitude. He said that he had never had a dad and he had learnt to live without one and he wasn't going to let it bother him now. He was glad that he had been told who his real dad was but he wasn't sure that it made a lot of difference as his dad didn't want to know him...With regard to whom Peter tells, it would seem that he has worked out who he can trust and who not to trust. I think the fact that when he talks about it he does so in an up-front unselfconscious manner must positively influence the way people respond to the information.'*

About her own feelings, Peter's social worker writes:

> *'Peter's matter of fact, philosophical acceptance of the situation is in keeping with his character as a whole. I was left feeling that it had been right to tell him about his origins, that he was able to accept and live with it as a part of himself that was alright. His*

*father would seem to be the one with the problem about this. It is
not possible to know what effect this knowledge may have had on
Peter in terms of his general sense of identity, self esteem and
sexuality. He has many problems but I believe that his difficulties
are due to his early deprivation, physical ill health, and the mental
and physical effects of this.'*

John and Andrew: (planned telling of brothers)

Both John and Andrew, now in their twenties, have many problems which
their adoptive mother believes relate more closely to their early multiple
experiences of separation and loss than to knowledge about their origins.
They continued to try to sort out their feelings about this. When their
father died, their adoptive mother wrote:

*'John felt quite dramatically about it all at first, but some time later
told me that thinking about it, the death of my mother meant more
to him than his father's because she had loved him for several years
and he had never really known his father. Actually going to the
funeral took quite a big effort for him and he came home to me and
went out and then came back to me.'*

And about the abuse of his sister:

*'His sister's experiences have further convinced Andrew that his
family were completely out of order (another of his phrases) and
even if one tried to understand what happened within his own
family, that his grandmother became ill and rather than look
outside the family the father turned to his eldest daughter, he thinks
this is absolutely wrong and he wants nothing to do with them.'*

The boys' adoptive mother sums up her own feelings as follows:

*'I know that I speak for both myself and John and Andrew when I
say that we are all very glad that they were told who their father
was, that they know the whole truth about their background and
that nothing any longer is kept back. John accepts that the timing
on this was right, when he was old enough to understand, and
within the love of the family, whereas Andrew thinks if they knew*

77

they should have told him.

'*It certainly made a big difference to me that there was nothing I knew that they did not. Personally I've always felt comfortable with the knowledge, but maybe it was easier for me as I was a social worker. What I did find hard in becoming a mother to them was their anger at "a mother" (which I knew related to their early deprivation) but which I thought was exacerbated by their lack of understanding as to why she had seemed to have abandoned them. I hoped that if they knew the reasons they would start coming to terms with it, to understand more of her situation, and therefore have less anger in their hearts to project onto me. I'm not sure that it worked from that point of view!*'

Jenny: (adolescent queries)

Although Jenny did not return to live with her foster family after the telling because her behaviour continued to be difficult, they steadily maintained links with her, and eight years later her social worker wrote:

'*I telephoned the foster mother and was greeted warmly and told that they were all well and that Jenny was married to a very nice man. She had been married from their house and given away by the foster father, she had a nice flat which she keeps beautifully and visits the foster home every weekend. She and her husband go on holiday with the foster parents.*'

The social worker arranged a visit and subsequently wrote:

'*Jenny is now an attractive, well-groomed, self-confident young woman, married to an apparently strong stable man a little older than her. I would not have known her...She found it difficult to separate the features in her story which related to incest to those which related to her getting to know her first mother and coping with all the problems at that time. There was more in the interview about her relationship with the two mothers than about the incest. She does think that children have a right to know the facts. She thinks that the age at which she was told, i.e. sixteen, was about right: "Twelve would be too young."*'

'She supposes that if a child is living with a family the foster mother would be the right one to tell her, if not, the social workers are quite suitable. She hardly ever thinks about it now but it is not buried and sometimes she and her husband discuss it if something comes up. She is not aware that there is a lot of talk about this kind of sexual abuse in the media; she has not noticed. She does not think being told upset her and she does not relate it to any of the difficulties she had during those two years. She would advise any young person wishing to get to know a natural family in those circumstances to think hard, but if they really wanted to she supposed it would be alright to meet them. She said that she had been thinking about her mother and the story that the incest had only happened once. She found that hard to believe and could not imagine why her mother had not protested and told someone; "she must have wanted it," she said. She also wondered if the grandmother must have known what was going on.

'More now than when she was visiting the birth family she expressed puzzlement about her father's attitude, not really understanding how he must feel. I offered some interpretation and explanation and asked her if she thought it would have helped if I had helped her mother to tell her what it had been like for her when Jenny was born. She said "No, they could never really communicate properly. It was not possible after so much time." My records tell a different story, that a warm relationship seemed to be developing. She told me that when she heard I had been in touch she thought it might be because her mother was wanting news. I asked her if she would mind if I got in touch with her mother to see how she was. She said no, but she feels uneasy in case her mother wants to get in touch. She says that she and her husband can only think that the foster parents who brought her up are her real parents and she does not want to belong in any way to her birth family.'

In retrospect the social worker comments:

'So many different things were going on in Jenny's life, from job searching and accommodation problems to the conflict of loyalties,

her boyfriend and his problems that it is difficult to separate them. Now she seems to see that this one fact (her origins) as standing on its own not particularly related to anything else, and not as important as many of the other things which have happened to her.'

9 Conclusions and implications for practice

This chapter draws together significant information that emerges from the available case studies and from the reported social work intervention. It goes on to offer a discussion about these in the context of the presentations in Chapters 1, 2 and 3. It then adopts a wider approach and, using the additional material from correspondence and contact during the life of the working party, points to the practice implications from this multidisciplinary material. These implications for practice are relevant for anyone – practitioner, carer or family member – involved in offering advice, support and intervention to any member of the different family networks that can become enmeshed in this area of taboos, secrets, myths and misconceptions.

The case studies
There are certain recurring themes running through these case studies. There are also some basic recurring facts that need to be considered and tied to the legal definitions and sanctions about incest. These provide some of the strands of the framework which any intervention, whether helping to formulate a plan or disclosing about origins, has to take cognisance of.

1 Legal issues
Incest as a criminal offence is defined differently in different countries. In the group we have studied the incestuous relationships were as follows:
– one was between siblings
– three were between daughter and biological father (four children were involved because two were brothers with the same parentage)
– one was uncertain, possibly between daughter and father or between siblings
– one was with an uncle

– two instances were with a stepfather who was therefore not biologically related. (There were three children involved here since this included twins)

As far as the law in the UK is concerned, the fact of incest in the first three groups would be seen as a criminal offence, both in England and Wales and in Scotland. However, the latter two would be interpreted differently north and south of the border: In England they are not criminal whereas in Scotland they are.

A further aspect which could exacerbate the dilemma facing the family and any professional counsellor are the legal considerations with regards to age of the birth mother. In half of the cases we described, the mother was under the age of 16 and so sexual intercourse would be a criminal offence, possibly leading to court proceedings, irrespective of the mother's relationship to the father.

2 Genetic issues

None of the ten offspring described in this study had a medical condition which was attributable to the close consanguinity of their birth parents. However, the possibility that this would be significant was a factor in keeping the incest a secret, as in Peter's case, or in wondering if it were significant when there were health problems as for Andrew. It also loomed large for Jack, whose impetus to search arose once he had become a father and had children of his own. The knowledge about the incest was a great shock to him and he and his wife were worried about the consequences for their children.

Amongst those with adolescent queries, Jenny coped well with learning about her origins, but then had to realise that others thought children of incest were always "mental". Isabel's reaction to birth information was relief to have the mystery resolved but she needed repeated reassurance about the implications for herself, that is, that she would not go mad because she was the child of relatives.

As far as carers or possible carers were concerned, there is evidence in the case studies that the genetic aspect was an issue for some of them, although it is not always possible to disentangle this from a more general abhorrence of incest and fear of the sexuality of the resulting children.

How valid the community's attitude is about the chance that the children will have disabilities or be "mental" is dealt with in Chapter 3 by Professor Raeburn. He makes it clear that in some very specific cases where there are autosomal recessive conditions the chances are greater than average. (Table 2 in Chapter 3 gives the commonest examples of autosomal recessive disorders.) In all others, no more than average. In quoting the work of Jancar and Johnston (see page 34 in Chapter 3), Professor Raeburn considers possible evidence as to whether there is a difference in the outcome depending on the form of incest, i.e. whether it is sibling, father/daughter or uncle/niece. There is no evidence either way.

What our work in this study showed us, however, was that these different relationships are viewed very differently. The sibling relationship gone too far is found to be more understandable and therefore acceptable than those between a daughter and father, niece and uncle, stepdaughter and stepfather. This could be because there could be seen to be some consenting equality between siblings. In other relationships, the adult is seen as carer and protector and therefore, in an incestuous situation, as exploiter. This leaves the practitioners and carers with a dilemma: how can they help the children of incest to understand their parents' inappropriate sexual behaviour, and to see that it is something quite separate from their own individual self-worth, while at the same time helping them to acknowledge that their parents' behaviour is not acceptable.

We conclude that at whatever stage a practitioner becomes involved, it is wise to disentangle the genetic facts from the myths. When doubt or latent fear is identified, the advice of a geneticist should be sought; Chapter 3 demonstrates the complexity of the genetic factors and expert advice is clearly necessary in assessing the risks and likely health outcome for each child. The fact that in this small reported study none of the ten children had cause for concern proves nothing about prevalence. The case material does, however, show that the levels of anxiety and fear engendered are way beyond the real risks.

3 Attitudes and relationships of the people around the children
The case histories map out well the complex early lives of these children

and how acceptance or rejection by their birth family depended not on them but on how people felt and reacted towards the adults who had created them.

There is only one example of sibling incest in this study. This is also the only example of a child spending his early childhood in his birth family, coming into care, being placed for adoption (at 11 years) and returning to the care of his birth family after the placement broke down. The follow-up contact suggested a good enough outcome for him. The fictitious example given by Professor Raeburn in Chapter 3 described a child remaining within the care of the birth family after sibling incest. No conclusions should be drawn from this. It is, however, illustrative of what the other histories also show, which is that adults' resentments, rejection and fear of criminality about the incest influence the way they can relate to the child and as a baby and a person who requires love and respect from adults.

The attitude of the carers is also crucial. There are clear instances of love and concern for these children, even though the carers were kept in the dark about the child's origins or given minimal information. Clearly, this information should have been shared with them. But that does not mean it ceases to be a problem for them. There are several examples of this in the study: Isabel's adoptive parents were committed to be open and honest and supportive about their daughter's race, culture and origins, but they could not manage the necessary openness about the incest; Peter's foster father saw every "misbehaviour" of the child in terms of his origins; John and Andrew's adoptive mother said she was glad that she had not told anyone about their incestuous origins when she needed support from her extended family during their adolescent difficulties. She was aware that she might not have got that help had they known, and all the blame could have been transferred to the incest which, of course, is not modifiable by environmental factors, love and kindness. The adult searcher, Marion, could see with hindsight that her adoptive mother knew more than she would admit to, but she also feared or was upset by it, either because of its content or how it affected her view of herself as a mother.

One of the problems for practitioners involved in developing individual care plans for these children is how to assess the carers' attitude to incest. The assessment must include not only their general attitude towards incest but also first, their feelings about the detailed history of this particular child, and second, how these feelings may evolve as the child reaches puberty and adult sexuality. In work with adoptive families it has long been established that parents who are ill at ease with their child's birth background can provoke, by their anxiety, the very behaviour that they fear. This may have contributed to the breakdown of Peter's placement following a preparation policy of openness with both Peter and the prospective permanent parents. (The examples given by the medical adviser member of the working party, and quoted in Chapter 2, illustrate vividly what can happen here.)

Attitudes of the children and young adults
For the children and young adults themselves except the adult searcher Jack, the general impression from all the studies is that the incest as such was not a serious problem. It was the feeling of betrayal at being lied to that had angered them. Even worse were occasions when there were conflicting stories or gaps that adults refused to fill. Jack's comments about this are very poignant:

'I feel in a worse dilemma now – an uncle who doesn't want to know me and a mother who has disowned me, but they both have different versions. I feel frustrated that it has always got to me. I never accepted that this was the end of the story. My heart says nobody rejects a baby for no good reason: I wouldn't myself.'

However, for those who were told by people with whom they had a trusting relationship, and if the "telling" was done sensitively depending on their needs and over time with follow-up support, the outcome appeared to be different. Typical comments were:

'Ah, that explains why my mother could not keep me.'

'That explains the secrecy that's been around.'

'That explains ... (some particular facet of their life or an incident that they reported that they did not understand).'

None of the young adults at follow-up regretted having been told. They were glad that they had been and they thought the age at which they had been told was about right – not too young yet old enough to understand. Those not told by foster carers with whom they had a good relationship felt that the latter should have been given the information and done the telling.

Two of the children in their teens needed help to work out what they wanted to share with other people and to consider the following:
- that they would be wise to recognise that not everyone would be accepting and understanding;
- that they did not need to tell everyone;
- that they had to think ahead as to who they could trust with the information and with whom they should use a simpler but honest and straightforward "cover story" to explain who they were.

The adoptive mother of John and Andrew made a revealing observation in this respect: 'It has always been clear to me that there would be certain people who just never would feel comfortable with the information.' She also gave examples of the difficulties of assessing which of her "liberal" friends would be accepting of the situation: 'It is easy to underestimate how much to the rest of the world it is a taboo subject.'

Was the difference in "social level" an issue for the young people themselves? In Chapter 5 we provided some basic facts about the families: the birth families were described as "working-class families"; the families into which the children were adopted were "middle class". The only reference to the difference in "social level" was made by Marion. She said that this worried her and she wondered if it would be a problem when she and her birth family met. They did meet and she did not report on that meeting; all she divulged was that upon also meeting her maternal grandmother, she now had two conflicting stories about her origins.

Intervention strategy: the telling process or how the barrier of secrecy was broken

For the adult searchers, they initiated their inquiries at points in their lives when this became important to them – Pat when she was getting married at 18; Marion when her adoptive parents had died and she no longer felt a sense of loyalty to them; Jack when he was married and had children and this compelled him to find out more.

Two of these searchers were supported by social workers. Jack was not. Jack's sense of shock at discovering about the incest was clearly described in Chapter 7: 'I was prepared for everything except incest.' Also clear was his feeling of frustration about the different stories and the gaps in his own history, his anxieties for his children and the consequent strains on his wife and their relationship: 'My wife is sympathetic, but she gets tired of it.'

One could argue that with counselling, help and support, some initial inquiries could have prepared him for the truth, reduced some of the uncertainties and conflicting versions and helped him to come to terms with his birth past.

The reports made by the social workers of their intervention work are best left to be read in full. The reader can thus sense how they were aiming to offer the facts but in such a way as to emphasise a positive interpretation of aspects of the parental figures without in any way implying that their behaviour was other than unacceptable. Exactly how much the listeners took hold of this is difficult to judge. None of them appeared to have felt incriminated by their parents' behaviour, although they were angry with either their mother or their father. For example, Andrew and John were not able to modify their view of their mother even after meeting her – evidence of deep feelings of rejection, which were clearly shared by Jack who talked of 'an uncle who doesn't want to know and a mother who has disowned me'.

The comments of the social workers about guarding over long periods a secret that they considered belonged elsewhere is an experience shared by many professionals. It is part of the confidential relationship that is the basis of all therapeutic intervention work. The dilemma, however, in these particular families is that the secret is about adults' "transgression" against sexual taboos and it is their belief that this is their secret, to keep or not as they choose; whereas professional knowledge is that children need this information to build up a true picture of themselves and who they are. The details in Chapter 2 give the literature and research study basis underpinning this knowledge.

It can be argued that some information is so potentially damaging and confusing that professionals may sometimes have to decide they are being inappropriately officious by offering it. If a secret can remain a secret, or if the recipient is so out of touch with reality or so limited in understanding, the benefit to be gained by them by offering them details of a secret which, in any case also belongs to others, can be questionnable. The equilibrium of a whole family network could be destroyed by such a revelation.

Clearly, the birth mother of the twins, Maria and Suzanne, feared such an upheaval and made the social worker promise not to tell the twins until after she had met them. In the end, of course, that resolved nothing in this particular case. Whatever the morality surrounding issues about whose secret it is and who has a right to keep personal information confidential to themselves, few secrets in families can remain secret. Something, someone, somewhere sparks off a sense of doubt; or gaps in a family history become intolerable and unacceptable and then the damage is done. Children feel deceived and some can react with the question 'What else have I been deceived about?'

When to tell
The histories show how circumstances determined when a decision was made by the social workers to intervene and tell the young people. The young adults stated that they felt the time of the telling was right in each of their individual lives. Certainly, those told in their teens learnt and understood the implications better than the adult searchers, Pat and Jack, who did not learn until they were adults. By that time, they had learnt all the attitudes of the community towards incest and no doubt had internalised these attitudes. By contrast, Jenny was quite excited by her discovery and wanted to tell everyone. She had to be counselled that not everyone would be understanding and that it was wise to have a less than full explanation of her origins to tell generally.

In the histories there are also instances in which the social worker or adoptive mother had to sense when it was "the right time to tell". The adoptive mother had to wait three years. The social worker of the twins set up a possible intervention time only for her efforts to be thwarted by the birth mother's insistence that the twins should not be told; the social worker had to then wait for another opportunity. Siblings present another difficulty for the teller. The twins' social worker waited for several years before she felt that both were ready simultaneously. In such a strategy of waiting there is always, of course, the possibility that an opportunity will not present itself or will not be taken and the information will never be given. So when appropriate opportunities present themselves, they have to be taken. A vivid example of this was in correspondence and telephone conversations during the time of the working party. A young girl had a child by her stepfather. When the child was still under school age the mother was about to marry and her husband would have then become the child's caring father. Should the young mother tell the child who her biological father really was? She thought long about it, but then the excitement of the wedding and her new life took over. The time to do it with a simple explanation had passed. Would another opportunity present itself or would it now be best left unsaid?

The right time to tell and how much detail to offer does not just relate to the age and stage of cognitive, social and emotional development of children but also to their awareness and acceptance of the sexuality of adults and of their parent figures. However, pre-school age children can understand simple factual information about themselves and their parentage if it is given in a straightforward way. There is no one right time to tell, but rather a process over time of being open, and offering information and explanations appropriate to the child's developing understanding and their particular pace and interest.

How to tell

The detailed reports of how the interviews were done show how the whole picture could gradually be presented; how it was based on first developing a relationship of trust and how the teller had taken time to think through and consider what incest really meant and what detail was relevant and what was erroneous, uncertain or irrelevant. In fact, all the social workers in the working party commented on how much easier it was to do than they had previously imagined. They were surprised at this and at how well the young people responded. Once the social workers got over their own hesitancy the young people listened quietly, although often avoiding eye contact, while the social workers carefully judged the pace at which to present the details, stopping to check back with the young person that they understood and were ready to move on. The questions from the young people came gradually over time.

What is described in the last paragraph exactly mirrors the experience in adoptive families when adoptive parents take the initiative and offer information about the birth family to their adopted son or daughter. These children, too, listen attentively but want to be offered more information and detail, while often feigning the indifference as was reported by the social workers in this study. (This one-way communication in adoptive families was discussed in Chapter 2.)

The fear of social workers about embarking on telling about incest is also commented on by Griffith, a counsellor from New Zealand: 'In my experience of meeting many hundreds of adoption "consumers" around the world, adopted people conceived by rape or incest do not normally fall apart when they find out, as many professionals fear. They often cope much better than the people who try to help them.'[1]

For those unsure of whether and when it is wise to embark on telling a young person, it is very helpful to discuss this with another experienced professional. There are two instances in our study where the tellers consulted with a child psychiatrist. Those working in that discipline and in clinical psychology are usually experienced in helping children to face and accept difficult facts about their parents or traumatic situations. They know from their experience of working over time with such children that it is better for the children to learn about family tragedies and grief rather than to be kept in ignorance, as if to protect them, or to pretend certain things had not happened.

What we learnt from the working group in our study was that social workers need support and constructive supervision from a professional colleague when they are involved in such intervention and afterwards. It is a very stressful piece of work to do and it should be recognised as such. The several quotes recorded by the social workers of how they personally experienced holding the secret and then being involved in sharing it with the children speak for themselves. For example, Peter's social worker said:

'Telling him turned out to be easier in the end than I expected. Like any secret, once it was spoken it just became much less awful. That is not to say I don't recognise that the burden has now been taken off my shoulders and put on to Peter who, after all, has to live with this for the rest of his life.'

The twins' social worker wrote:

'I should have told the girls the whole story whatever their mother said. Shielding them from part of it was wrong. They would have needed help in handling so much at once but they could have coped...I kept the secret of their paternity for several years and was not happy in my mind about this...I do not believe they would have approached the agency for information and I therefore felt myself to be the sole possessor of a secret that was really theirs.'

The adoptive mother who was also a social worker and who had kept the secret for three years wrote:

'The marvellous thing is that it is now out in the open, that we are all feeling pretty comfortable with it...It's no big deal...For my part, the best thing is that I no longer know something that they don't know; it's as if we are walking about in the sunshine and fresh air, instead of boxed in a room with a cupboard that is about to disgorge some terrible taboo secret.'

Social workers' reflective comments

All five tellers were experienced, confident social workers, three of them well known to and trusted by the young people. But only two of them were in a position to allow the young people (the two brothers and the 25-year-old twin girls) to indicate the timing for the telling. The disruptive behaviour of the two adolescent girls, however, may have indicated their need to know.

In every case, the tellers felt that they possessed a secret to which they had no right and most of them admitted to a feeling of relief when the secret was shared with the people to whom they felt it belonged. One of the social workers wondered if she had shifted a burden on to her young client. They all seemed to consider that the secret belonged to the child rather than to the parents. In the case of the twins, the mother's request not to tell was respected at first, but only because this was the only condition on which she would agree to see the girls and this was considered to be their most pressing need at the time. Only Peter's birth mother gave her agreement before the event, but the birth mothers of the brothers and of Jenny agreed with the telling after the event.

During our extensive discussions none of the tellers expressed personal revulsion at the concept of incest, but they were all acutely conscious of the incest taboo in our society. Most of them agreed that their most difficult task was to marry their non-judgmental explanation of how the incest had occurred with an explanation of why the young people should not discuss their origins outside the circle of those who knew.

With the exception of Pat, all the young people were at some time critical of their mother's sexual behaviour, even when it was clear that she herself had been abused. In the case of the brothers, this feeling persisted despite their adoptive mother's sympathy for their birth mother.

In at least one case, and possibly in others, a network of incestuous relationships existed within the family and it was difficult for the young women involved to extricate themselves. During the project we heard of such a network extending to three branches of a family and encompassing a family business. The young woman we spoke to, who was probably born of incest and had been abused by various male relatives, suffered a breakdown when she left home and is still afraid of travelling anywhere alone. Young women like this grow up accepting their family's mores as normal and may even be protected from social contact with the outside world by the companionship of peers within the family and by employment within the family enclave. For those that do escape, the culture clash must be devastating, as too their feeling of isolation from all those whom they previously knew.

The implications for practice

This study shows how social workers need to use knowledge and expertise from other disciplines. The material presented in the case histories and the detailed recording of the intervention interviews also clearly defines the area of social workers' professional practice and expertise. They deal with individuals in complex family and social situations. They understand the dynamics of personal and family inter-relationships and can set these against the background of societal attitudes, perceptions, prejudices and notions and the harsh realities of the material world within which adults who are parents have to provide for the basic needs of their children. For every child born of incestuous relationships all the issues in any child care referral must be considered, together with the powerful reaction and views of everyone to incest (using the term not as a general descriptive term for child sexual abuse, but meaning full sexual intercourse between prohibited relatives). Anyone involved with these children – counsellors, social workers, doctors, lawyers, members of the police force or of the judiciary – has to come to terms with the complexities surrounding incest and their own irrational fears and attitudes to these. A crucial question to consider is whose interests are they serving, a question to be explicit about and to resolve. The authors' view is that all decisions must take as the bottom line what is likely to be in the best long-term interests of these children throughout their childhood and adult life. No one, of course, can predict the ultimate outcome, but the hazards and alternative scenarios can realistically be addressed.

The points at which professionals may become involved with such families are:

– When the mother is pregnant and is very young. Perhaps we need more often to consider with very young mothers the possibility of incest. If it exists, it is likely to be denied and will be well hidden. If it is established as incest, there are medical and genetic issues that need to be resolved. This may lead to a decision by the mother to seek an abortion, but she may decide otherwise, or she may seek help too late. The chances of an abnormal foetus were spelt out in Chapter 3.

Birth mothers will almost inevitably feel vulnerable and have extremely mixed feelings regarding their child's parentage. There will be multiple reasons for this: the mother's sense of having been abused by the child's father or her reluctance to betray someone she cares for; the fact that she may blame herself for her child's conception; the fact, so evident from the case histories, that she is likely to have been rejected at least at some point by her family; lastly, the existence of the incest taboo in the community. When there have been criminal proceedings against the father, with its attendant publicity, her feelings of guilt and ostracism from other members of her family are likely to be even more acute.

– When the child is born and realistic plans have to be made for the child's long-term care. It has to be asked which are the birth families and their networks which will offer support and acceptance for the child for its own sake. What does not appear to go away, although it may alter over time, is how the adults deal with their own anger, guilt and feelings of betrayal.

The question to be asked is can they separate these off from how they feel about the child who, of course, is not responsible for his or her birth parents' behaviour.

– When a care plan already established has to be revised because of changed circumstances or because it breaks down. An outside person will then become involved. Earlier in this chapter we discussed the professional's duty to assess what is known about the carer's attitude, not only to children but towards a history of a birth family which has transgressed sexual taboos. Part of this assessment will be the cultural and religious concepts and beliefs already described (Chapter 1). It must be accepted that many people feel threatened by incest and sexual taboos but with support, education and personal counselling, many may be able to change their attitudes. Such change, as we have seen, is necessary in the long term. However, not all can live comfortably with incest.

This question should be addressed whenever a child born of incest becomes the responsibility of a social work, medical or legal agency. In the majority of cases, especially as far as doctors and lawyers are concerned, this will be in the form of helping birth parents towards an understanding of the issues involved and ensuring that they have adequate support in their task. This could extend in a few cases to acting as the parents' agent in the telling, as Isabel's social worker felt should have happened in her case. The experience of other young people in the project indicates, however, that they saw those with whom they lived, whether birth parent, adoptive parent or foster carer, as the teller with whom they would have felt most comfortable.

Carers who may have learnt at a later date about their foster child's origin, may be prey to strong feelings about the incest taboo and are likely to resent deeply the secrecy that an agency or individual social worker has imposed on them. They should know the facts from the start and it is they who are in the best position to tell the children about their origins and to reassure them. However, they may well need support, professional advice about the genetic aspects, and consultations with a professional about the emotional and social stage of development that their foster child has reached. Telling is not simply about a cognitive exercise; more significantly it is about emotional awareness and understanding of family relationship patterns. Continuing support and reassurance is likely to be needed over a considerable time concerning these issues, both for themselves and for the foster child.

In the long run, the more thought and care that is taken at the early stages, the better it will be for the child. However, there are enough clearly defined hurdles in the life cycle of these families to show the need of counselling and clinical genetic services to be readily available.

The value of post-placement adoption counselling services is becoming recognised, although not all areas of the UK have this available. Social workers providing these services should have sufficient expertise and experience in interpersonal relationship work with alternative families to be able to offer the type of counselling or consultation likely to be needed by and for these children. The counsellors too, however, will need to address their own attitudes towards incest.

The clear message from this study is that with appropriate knowledge of the true situation and a willingness to understand and accept the prejudices of others, but not to be swamped by the prejudices of others, these children need not live in the shadow of unspoken family secrets. On the other hand, it has also to be accepted that many seemingly "liberal-minded" carers and professionals cannot easily take on board fully the non-judgmental attitudes towards incest that are essential for a child's well-being. Failure to achieve this may produce a kind of abhorrence which persistently recurs within quite ordinary situations of family living. It is important to be aware of this and to accept it.

This is not then counselling work that *all* social workers/counsellors/ child psychiatrists can do, but many more could learn to do so. We consider that this study has contributed to enabling pracitioners to make this start by demolishing the myths surrounding incest and presenting facts and knowledge from which professionals can draw insights and guidance for their practice.

Reference

1 Griffith, K, Access to Adoption Records: The Results of the Changes in New Zealand Law, in (ed) Mullender, A, *Open Adoption: The philosophy and the practice*, BAAF, p 157, 1991.